Earliest picture of the whole family

**Mum, Dad, Chris and Me.
1939**

It's A Funny Old Life!

By

Michael B. Hatton B. E. M.

Preface

I suppose I must be one of the luckiest people to be alive! Anyhow, that's how I feel now. Of course, there have been times when I didn't feel this way. These occasions have been several and varied, and I will try to recount some of these in this publication. I will attempt to be reasonably accurate, but please allow some poetic licence, memories alter over the years. As suggested in the title, I will put more of an accent on the humorous side of my life, which has been spent as an agriculturist, or farmer! I have tried to follow a logical sequence, but in some instances have failed miserably. Please be a little tolerant.

Mum aged 2

Earliest pictures
of Mum,
Irene Edith
Marshall.
and
Dad,
Thomas Hatton

CONTENTS

Chapter 1

So This Is Farming - The scene is set.

My memories of farming really began when my family moved to a small farm near Nailsworth in the county of Gloucestershire. Before then I had really only been a small boy helping his Dad. The hills in this area are steep, and, bearing in mind that the year is 1950, motor vehicles were few and far between! I remember that first day, as I walked up the steep and winding road to our farm in Wallow Green, how beautiful this location was. I had travelled from school in Stroud by bus, and then had a two mile walk to home. The smell of the warm, wet hedgerows is still with me to this day. I had left behind at school, an afternoon of turmoil and frustration, where bullying was the accepted practice, not by pupils, oh no! This was the accepted practice for the teachers. It was from these afternoons of tension that I found the blessed relief of my solitary walk home.

It was on one of these meanderings homeward that I had my first encounter with an irate cow! I, in a world of my own, strolling along the footpath that was a shortcut to our farm, was so enraptured with the beauty of nature that I started to whistle as loud as I could. After several minutes of this, no doubt, terrible noise, I suddenly became aware of a rumbling and moaning noise. Being a sharp lad, I looked up, to see a very large red and white Ayrshire cow with enormous horns, approaching at great speed, at this time I had no experience of dealing with cows, so decided my best option was to vacate the field as fast as possible. It is at times like this that one seems to find hidden strength. I was always looked upon as a rather weak and feeble child, but I think, had my parents seen me, they would have been most impressed. I crossed the hundred yards or so at a speed that would have impressed the best athlete, and cleared the Cotswold stone style with feet to spare. This was really the first time I had used my legs to their full potential, and I found that I really quite enjoyed the experience, although I could certainly do without Daisy's help!

When we arrived in the Cotswold's, I was at the tender age of twelve, and I enjoyed working, during all my spare time, with my father on the farm. I had little experience of pleasure of a social kind. After we had been living there for some weeks, I was approached by some local boys and girls, and asked if they could play cricket in our field. I asked Dad, and he willingly agreed, so long as we didn't cause any damage. We all cut the grass, cleared the pitch of bovine excrement, and set up the stumps. We enjoyed our game for half an hour or so, and all sat down for a deserved rest. One of my new found friends, called Cathy, sat next to me and put her hand on the top of my leg. She was a gentle soul, with golden curls, that fell in ringlets round her red cheeked face. I had liked the look of Cathy, and would like to know her better. No girl had ever done this to me before, and I was slightly taken aback. However, I did quite like the experience, and I moved to encourage closer and more intimate contact. It had seemed so natural as we fumbled, and I was greatly aroused. It was at this crucial point that my Gran appeared at the gate to enquire as to what we were doing. This was, for many years, to be the story of my life, with Gran always somehow spoiling things. Whether this was by accident or design, I never really knew, but I suspect the latter. It was to be some time before I experienced these awakenings again.

One of my first memories of involvement with cows is milking three or four cows before going to school. This was the 1950's; no milking machines then, a three legged stool, a bucket, and a cap on back-to-front! Two reasons for the cap, cows produce a large amount of grease from their flanks, and although Brylcreem was in fashion, the bovine pong was not. Also, at springtime, cows often had mites; it was not an unusual sight to see milkers scratching like lunatics! Cows can be of an unpredictable nature, and many are the times that a poohy foot was placed in the bucket I was filling. The main thing was not to loose the milk, remove the foot, carefully, if possible, and carry on milking. There were occasions when an irate animal would decide she'd had enough of being milked, then bucket, stool, cowman and cap would end up strewn across the cowshed. Happy days!

It was on one of these temperamental occasions that whilst doing my preschool milking, that a very large bovine foot was placed unceremoniously in my nether regions, causing extreme discomfort. Times were not easy along then, and I was wearing my only pair of school trousers. Well, the stain can be minimized, but the aroma remains, I smelt like a cow for the rest of that day, and had a lonely dinner hour.

I began to enjoy the outdoor life, and its many opportunities for learning practical skills. All the field boundaries in this area at that time were Cotswold dry stone walls, and wayward cattle, not to mention children kept me in full time weekend employment rebuilding these barriers. My first attempts were, to put it mildly, abysmal. Some did stay up overnight, but the worst fell as I left the field. Practice makes perfect, and I had plenty of practice! Eventually they did stay up, although the appearance was not good. With more time, and a lot of profanities, they looked good and stayed up. I find satisfaction and mental relaxation when building stone walls.

One very great advantage of living on a farm is the many various opportunities that are available to a child. In these modern days it is not possible for young people to obtain this experience, as Health and Safety will not allow them to venture into the farmyard, but I am sure that they are very much the losers, and they miss out on so much that would equip them to deal with life's problems. Along with milking and stone walling, there were tractors. I dearly wanted to drive the tractor, not one of these modern things; this was a Fordson, complete with starting handle, and of unpredictable temperament. These tractors were started using petrol, and then, when the engine was warm, were turned onto paraffin. If the engine was idling for sometime, then it cooled down and started misfiring. It had only one foot pedal, the first part was the clutch, the lower part was supposed to be the brake! The seat was an iron dish on a spring, there were no cabs with heaters then, you sat in all weathers, soaking up sun, rain, sleet, snow, everything that nature could throw at you. Looking back, I cannot for the life of me see, why I wanted to drive that monstrosity. But, I did and Dad said I couldn't drive it until I could start it. What a challenge! I spent hours trying to start that tractor. It had an unreasonable habit of "kicking back", which meant that if you pushed the handle round too slowly, the engine fired early and tried to go backwards. This idiosyncrasy caught many an unsuspecting tractor driver unaware and was responsible for many a broken wrist. As I grew older and stronger, lo and behold, one day the tractor roared into life and I was away.

Our farm was rather isolated, and the milk produced from Daisy and her friends was mostly collected at the farm gate. However, in bad weather it was our responsibility to get this precious liquid to a main road at Horsley. Milk was our only produce and our only income, so it was vital to deliver it to a collection point. Our only vehicle was a Morris 10cwt. Light van, circa 1938. By today's standard, she was an ugly beast. She had been hand painted a pale shade of green, a very square box, two back doors and a thermometer on top of the silver coloured radiator. She had a dubious temper, and although seldom let us down completely, was known on occasions to show, shall we say, "a female tendency" towards unpredictability." Here again, a starting handle was the only method of getting her going, and, as she was really only used in inclement or disgusting weather conditions, often many swear words and curses were uttered before she decided to oblige. As she was used more in one bad winter, the clutch started slipping. We had forty gallons of milk on board, and as first gear was a higher ratio than reverse, we thought we would try backing up the offending hill. Wonder of wonders, it worked, and for many months it was not unusual to see our green Morris reversing up the steepest hills. At some later occasion, while trying to hone my skills with a catapult, that our beloved van had it's left back window shattered, and henceforth had a piece of plywood in it's place. I think that the van window was the only thing I ever hit with my catapult!

My brother was older than me by four years, and so had already left school by this time and milked the cows and carried out most of the day to day tasks on the farm with Dad. He enjoyed the country life, especially the country girls! He also had rather a liking for field sports, and was a good shot with a twelve bore. Somehow, the field sports and liking for girls was his downfall. Whilst out shooting pigeons, with his girlfriend, he managed to shoot his big toe. He made a very clean job of it, and after a few days in hospital came home, although being rather incapacitated for some weeks. This meant that my duties were expanded, and I arose earlier in the mornings, and milked as many cows as possible before walking the two miles to catch the school bus. We never did get to the bottom of how my brother amputated his big toe, but we felt that somehow, his girl friend was involved. Today, in similar circumstances, the occurrence would make headline news, but at that time, all farms had at least one shotgun, and licenses were easily obtained. I now had to drive the tractor, and also became much faster at milking. This was, of course, to the detriment of my school work. Homework became secondary to my farm jobs, and I am afraid, was often of a rather scrappy nature.

The Cotswold's have beauty and splendour enough to satisfy the sternest critic, but one thing about them is that in winter, there seemed always to be a significant fall of snow on at least one occasion. It was in a particularly cold snap that three or four inches of snow fell during the afternoon. My special friend, as Cathy had become and I made a, quite useful, sledge, and went off over the fields to Horsley where the roads and meadows are steep. It was possible at this time to not see a vehicle all day, so the idea of a road accident was unthinkable. We spent hours sledging down the hills, and then dragging the thing back up again. We had great fun frisking in the snow, we didn't notice the cold. It was a clear evening, and with the moon reflecting off the snow, we were able to see till quite late. By the time Cathy and I returned home, it was very late, and teatime long since past, but those were different times, and there was no panic or worry. It was a day that has stuck in my mind vividly, and a never to be forgotten afternoon, hopefully for Cathy as well.

I have mentioned that this was a rural location, and the facilities were also of the rural kind. The toilet was a bucket under a wooden plank, with a hole of dimensions suitable for an average bottom to fit, more or less comfortably. The said "convenience", was located in a small square tin shed. This shed was no doubt for hygiene reasons, situated some distance from the back door of the house. To reach this building, it was necessary to attire oneself in warm clothing, and put on wellies. This I found a little tiresome and seeing that the toilet was, in fact, only three or four yards from the lounge window, I used to stand on the windowsill, and take a shortcut through the lounge window. This was frowned upon by the more mature members of the family and I was told to stop doing this. Needless to say when nobody was about, this was my preferred route. It was sometime later that I came into the lounge, just in time to see Dad coming back through the window. For sometime after this, until an indoor toilet was installed, we all used this route, unless we had visitors, it just seemed difficult to explain, opening a window and saying, "I'm just going to the toilet". Of course, whatever was put into the bucket in the tin shed, also had to be removed! Volunteers were few and far between. When it became neccasary to beat the flies off the toilet before you could sit down, something had to be done. The frequency of emptying not as regular as it should have been. However, the depository for the contents of said bucket was a trench at the bottom of the garden. This was our bean trench, and the beans we grew there were a sight to behold!

As we lived two miles from Nailsworth, and this was our nearest food shop, we did not make this steep excursion very often, we had only the Morris, which was mostly too much trouble to start, or we walked. In those gentler times, bread, groceries, butchery and a hardware van called weekly. We had no mains services, no mains water, electricity or telephone. Water was from a well, via a hand pump, lighting was a paraffin lamp, with a mantle. Strangely enough, either our eyesight was much better then, or we were just used to these, what appear now to be, very dim lights. We also had a travelling library, fortnightly, and the dark winter evenings were spent, either reading or playing ping pong!

During the long summer evenings, I often walked with Dad, over the beautiful hills and soft meadows. I still remember the sweet scent of the hay, drying in the fields. It was really my first chance to get to know him. He had joined the army in 1939, when I was nine months old and I didn't see him until I was six. He had spent a lot of the war years in Burma, and I suppose, although I didn't realize it at the time, was quite stressed for several years after, and even more so in his later years. At that time there was no counselling, and everyone just got on with life and coped as best they could. In the six years since his demob, he had been working hard laying concrete paths and roadways for all the new houses that were being built at that time, to earn enough money to buy a smallholding. This he had achieved and the progression from that was the small farm here. So, what with work, moving and buying land, I had not been in a position to find out much about him. At six years old, this man, who I was told was my Dad, returned from his traumatic war experiences. He, at that time, never mentioned the time spent abroad. However, during these long walks over the hills and valleys, with the scent of the sweet hay, and hedge blossom, strong in our nostrils, we talked and we learnt much about each other. It was a never to be repeated, but never to be forgotten experience.

While we were living at the farm, mains electricity and mains water was being spread much farther than the towns and villages that had, up until then, been the only beneficiaries. They both arrived at a similar time, the spring of 1951, and there was indeed much excitement about their arrival. The electricity was the first to be connected, and as it was Easter holidays, I spent most of the time "helping" the electrician. I learnt much from this and in later years, I was able to install electricity on another farm. Now we had an electric light in the cowshed! With the brighter lights at night, we could see things that we hadn't seen before! Whole new vistas were opened up for us. We had, when we came here, a wireless, later called radio, but it used accumulators, and batteries, which were seldom replaced, but now, oh joy! We had an electric radio. We were now able to listen to radio shows, news, music, all at the turn of a switch. Could life get any better?

The mains water had to wait for connection, as finances were not available. It was connected during the school summer holidays, and I then became a plumbers mate, learning all that I could about water pipes, fittings and how to put threads on galvanized pipes. As can be realized from the previous ramblings, I was much more interested in what was happening on the farm, than in my school work. I am afraid this suffered badly, but, looking back, I think that the practical experiences that I obtained have been of much more use than some of the academical ones that I neglected.

I did have two good friends at school, Anthony and Martin, Anthony was of a similar ability to me, and we enjoyed completing our lessons together on the school playing field during the lunch break. Martin was a much better scholar, and seemed to pick up things much quicker than we did. I suppose now that most of my thoughts were of what was occurring on the farm. On arrival home after school, I would first visit Chris or Dad to hear what had happened during my absence. I would then visit any new arrivals, calves, piglets or even a new clutch of chicks. While I was carrying out these inspections there would be a loud call from Mum, "come and change your clothes". Needless to say, by this time I had knelt or sat in something disgusting. Boys haven't changed much in that department!

I had a good soprano voice, my voice broke quite late, and I enjoyed singing in the Marling School choir. During my last term we practiced every evening so that we could sing at the Three Choir festival, unfortunately, we moved to another farm before it was due, so I was unable to attend.

Me aged nine, in front of home made block wall

Chris with the offending gun, Fooks Farm, Nailsworth

Chris, Me, Dad 1960

Me 13, Whitmore Farm

Chapter Two

Moving On!

It was on a cold Mayday in 1952 that it happened. Dad and my brother, had decided that we needed a larger farm, especially as it appeared that I would be joining them when I left school. We had been farming 28 acres at Nailsworth, and they had found a 52 acre farm on the edge of the Forest of Dean, situated between Longhope and Mitcheldean. The estate agents described the farm as "Green pasture on a gentle slope, running down to a sparkling stream, with mature and productive orchards. The house was in need of modernization". My description would be "Rough grazing land on the side of a mountain, running down to a dirty ditch with ancient and useless apple trees and the house in need of a bulldozer". This was my first impression, and it didn't change over the three years that we were there. Really, the reason that Dad purchased this property was that it was affordable from the sale of the smaller property. The house and buildings were set at the top of the hill, with most of the land falling away to the front. The views were magnificent, and it was said that if you could see May Hill, it was going to rain, if you couldn't see it, then it was raining. This was pretty well true!

We arrived in three cattle trucks, and of course, the Morris 10cwt. Light van. The first cattle truck contained the cows, the second, the equipment, and the third one had our furniture in it. The Morris van contained my Dad, Mum, Gran, Chris and myself, also in the back was three cats and our dog Judy, and various items of personal equipment, thrown in at the last moment. When we left Nailsworth, there had been a late fall of snow, and there had been about six inches at the top of the hills. On arrival at Longhope, the sun was shining, and there was grass in the fields. Could this be a good omen? As we unloaded the cows, there was great excitement amongst them, they could smell the grass, and knew that the time had come for their annual springtime release from a winter indoors. On lowering the cattle truck tailboard, there was a frantic stampede, and, although these animals were used to hills, this was somewhat steeper than they had previously encountered. Eighteen milking cows and four yearlings careered down this "gentle slope" at a rate of knots that was a wonder to behold. This was fine until the ones in front realized that they were running out of field, and the fence at the boundary of the "sparkling stream" was becoming ever closer. The ones in front, using remarkable four wheel braking techniques, which left four long strips of removed turf flying through the air. The problem was that the ones behind were still trying to catch up with the front runners. They achieved this somewhat faster than they expected when the front line stopped. Each cow weighing about half a ton, was travelling at say twenty miles an hour, then hitting more animals of a similar size, created a force that few fences could withstand. There was much complaining from the front rank as they were used like a battering ram. It goes without saying that the fence was in poor repair, and it suddenly became in much poorer repair as it disappeared into the "sparkling stream", out the other side and across the field of an unknown neighbour. I still think that this may, for some inconceivable reason, be why we never got on well with the fellow.

We retrieved our wayward animals eventually and had then to persuade them that it would be a great idea if they came into the shed to be milked. We did actually cajole two of the older ladies into the shed, but the remainder were adamant that this was not their scene at that moment. Between these trials and tribulations, the furniture had to be unloaded; we achieved this in a sort of piecemeal way. Animals come first and that is a fact that any farmers wife will agree with, so the furniture ended up in the yard, because the cattle trucks had to leave to be ready for an early market trip the following day. It was past midnight when we finally erected the beds and fell in, tired, irritable, hungry and fully clothed.

The following day we all awoke at our usual time of six thirty or thereabouts. It was a grand day, sun shining, birds singing, God was in his Heaven, all's right with the world! We were by now starving; Mum had found the necessary ingredients for a fry up, so while this was happening, Dad, my brother Chris and I went to see the "girls". We had left some hay in the yard overnight, in the hope that this would entice them in. Wonder of wonders, it had worked. The yard was full of contented cows. Fresh spring grass, eaten by a cow, does not entirely satisfy them; it tends to hasten their digestion and passes through, in a consistency that resembles green paint. Indeed, there are not many things that satisfy a cow more, than to attempt to paint cowshed, buckets and cowman. The said paint is exuded under pressure, either with a cough or a stretch; it travels horizontally until it strikes an immovable object. To combat this, fibre in the form of hay was fed; this slows down the process significantly. The yard gates were closed to ensure that the ladies did not leave, and then we fed ourselves. I still remember the taste of that wonderful food. I am sure that food has been just as good since, but that is an occasion when it really hit the spot!

The Farm

The farm was approached via a steep track that was not in good repair. It was really only suitable for four wheel drive vehicles, lorries, and of course, our Morris 10 cwt. Light van. I walked down this way to catch the school bus. I was thirteen, I had attended six different schools previously and I certainly was not looking forward to my days at the Grammar School in Cinderford. I think now, that moving from school to school as I had to, as we went from farm to farm, did not enhance my education. Each school has different teaching methods, different rules and regulations and by this time, all I really wanted was to stay home and help on the farm. My marks certainly went downhill, and most of my thoughts were at home.

The bus that was used for the school run was a normal service bus. At the time I did not think the noise excessive, but when I travel on a school bus today, I realise just how rowdy we were. I don't think that we were less noisy, just that when you are young, you don't hear it. We had a double decker bus, so most of us went upstairs, just as the youngsters do today. There was always much tutting from adults, but then old people always complain about the young. Not a lot changes there. There were some good times at school, but they were few and far between. I do remember that I became "very friendly" with one of my female friends and it was then that the journey home on the school bus became a joy. On my return journey in the afternoon I would stay on the bus past our farm entrance, and continue for another mile or so. This gave me a little more time with the girls. I then had a long walk up to our farm, but it was across fields and much nicer than the stony roadway.

I have said that the farm was on the edge of the Forest of Dean, indeed, the Forest was the farm boundary on one side. Mostly, this wasn't a problem, but there are lots and lots of sheep that roam these woodlands and rough grazing areas. After we had been at Longhope for a while, we were approached by a local dealer, to ask if we would take some sheep on "half crease", this meant that he would supply the sheep; we would feed and otherwise tend them. In return, we would be given half the sale price of all lambs sold and half the wool return. As we had not enough milking cows to graze the fields properly, this seemed a most acceptable idea. In due course, approximately a hundred in lamb ewes appeared. By the next morning, they had disappeared! The hunt was on. It was obvious from a quick inspection of the fences that they had decided to go for a ramble in the Forest. Several thousand acres of it. Well! They had to be found. We hadn't ventured far from home before in this wild and very overgrown area. There is one good thing with sheep and to me it is about the only good thing. It is that they stay together as a flock, mostly. One hundred sheep travelling through brambles and thickets, leave a very tell tale track, mostly of their wool. We followed for miles and miles and eventually found them grazing contentedly on the outskirts of Cinderford, this being a distance of five or so miles. I had a wonderful little dog at that time, her name was Judy and we spent every moment I was home together. She was a lifesaver that day and with our, slight assistance; we returned the wayward animals to their meadow. We later found out that the dealer had bought the sheep from a market for Forest sheep; they had no idea what good grass was, and did not really ever understand why we needed fences. The animals had returned to the same area that they had come from before being sold at the market.

Lost Sheep!

It was a few months later, as lambing started, that the sheep decided to go on walkabout again. It was a particularly cold winter, there had been a very heavy fall of snow and it covered everything in a beautiful white blanket. It had been a very cold night and the 2 am lambing inspection round had been a particularly unpleasant affair. I remember this, because I did it! There had been some problems, a set of backward twins and one lamb with its front legs back. These are normal problems that I learnt to deal with very quickly. On this occasion, the temperature was well below freezing, an exceedingly cold breeze was blowing from the north, the sort of wind that blows through, rather than round you. I finished the inspection and, as it was so cold, I took the little twins indoors and put them in the oven of the kitchen range. This is normal practice, as the range is shut down overnight, the oven cools to about blood heat and is ideal for reviving frozen lambs or calves. During cold windy weather, animals congregate on the leeward side of a hedge, where it can be several degrees warmer. As I fell back wearily into bed a thought crossed my mind, I had looked all along the hedge where I knew they would be sheltering and had assumed that I had seen them all, but, there had not been quite as many as I had expected. Well! It was gone three in the morning, so I thought; we would be out there with them again in a couple of hours. I fell asleep. It was general practice, that whoever did the 2 am watch was aloud to stay in bed until seven.

When I awoke I was greeted by the news that twenty or so sheep were missing in the Forest. I dressed in all the warm and weather proof clothing I could find, I knew there would be no school, as all the roads were impassable. I set off to assist. Dad and Chris had already left with Judy, some time before me, and the sheep's tracks and theirs, were easy to follow. By now we had been in this area on several occasions and I knew it quite well. Or so I thought! All went nicely to start with and I had been walking some time through the woods, when I realised that I hadn't been in this area before. I convinced myself, sort of, that all was well and if I followed the sheep tracks, I would find either the sheep, or Dad and Chris. It didn't quite work out like that. I found the sheep that I had been tracking, but they were not ours. It is surprising, all sheep look alike to most people, but when working with them on a daily basis, they become familiar and you know each animal as an individual. These were not our sheep! What to do now? I was thirteen, in the middle of an enormous area of forest; I didn't have Judy, as she always knew her way home. I tried to retrace my tracks, but there were so many, that it wasn't possible. I hadn't taken notice of which direction I had been travelling, nor, particularly of the surroundings, as I had been following their tracks. The snow was nearly up to my knees in places, and was over the top of my wellies, my feet were wet and very cold. I thought, I must not panic, think it out logically, which way is the sun? I looked up at the leaden sky, no idea! Which way is the wind? In the middle of a forest, no idea! So I did the next best thing and panicked. Not a big panic you understand, just a little one. I found a track that had been cut as a fire prevention lane, and decided to follow it. This was really quite a good idea, as all the fire lanes lead off of the main track through the Forest. After some time, possibly half an hour or so, I came to the edge of the Forest. I had been walking the wrong way! I reluctantly turned to retrace my steps and eventually came to the main track. I knew my way from here, or so I thought. It was one of those times when you feel really pleased with yourself for being so very clever, but when you are older, you know that something will go wrong! It did! I followed the main track until I recognised the side track that led to our fields. Have you noticed just how much things look the same under a foot of snow? I did come out into a field, but it wasn't our field, it could have been anywhere. I was tired, hungry, and cold, wet and felt very sorry for myself. I didn't know what to do; I stood and shouted very loudly, Judy! Judy! Judy! In a forlorn hope. I must admit, though it does pain me to say it, I had tears in my eyes. Perhaps it was the cold. I sat on a fallen tree and I panicked again. This was a much better one, full blown howling! I really had no idea what to do. I was too tired to retrace my steps and what was the point, I didn't know where I was when I got back there anyway. As I tried to calm down, I put my head in my hands and wondered what to do. After several minutes I decided that something was better than nothing, so started to stand up. As I did so, I saw, at my feet, but on the other side of the fallen tree, JUDY! I wept buckets! When she had arrived, or where she had come from, I had no idea. I must admit, I was quite pleased to see her.

I stood up, after giving her a little hug and said home Jude, she led the way. It turned out that I had only been three fields away from our land, but I had ended up in the fields of our neighbour with whom we had little contact and I did not recognise it. When at last I arrived home, it was a little disappointing. I was greeted with tales of how my Dad and Chris had found the sheep after being lost for ages. No one was really interested in my adventures. I found out later, that as soon as they had returned the wayward sheep, Judy had disappeared and they couldn't find her anywhere. I said no more, gave Judy a hug, and a portion of my dinner, I thought she had earned it!!

Lost Water Supply!

I have mentioned previously that the house left a little to be desired, to be more accurate; it left very much to be desired! It was built into the side of the hill, thus to level the floors, the ground floor was about four feet below ground level at the back, and eight feet above ground level at the front. Beneath the higher end, was an area we called the cellar. We used this as a room for relaxing in with working clothes and wellies on.   We had kettle and cups, so could make a brew!   On the floor above, the ground floor was a room where Gran slept, and a kitchen come living room, which was only ten feet by twelve feet, where we lived, ate, and listened to the radio in the evening.   My Brother, Gran and Dad, all smoked heavily and by bedtime, I almost had to cut a hole through the smoke to go to bed.   There were two rooms on the first floor, Mum and Dad had one, and Chris and I had the other.   When Mum's parents came to stay, Chris and I slept on the floor.   Looking back now, times were really hard and I don't know how Mum coped.

The water supply came from a field at the top of the farm, and came down the pipe by gravity.   Well this was supposed to be what happened!   The supply was intermittent, to put it politely.   After we had been at the farm for a month or so, the supply ceased completely.   We went up the field to investigate, and found the pipe blocked with frogs spawn.   We cleared it away, and went to see if that had solved the problem.   No such luck!   We decided to dismantle some of the pipe work at strategic intervals.   This was not easy, as we had no idea where the pipes went under ground.   After digging many holes, the fields resembled First World War battlefields!   We still hadn't located the pipe.   It was after excavating many such holes, that I had an idea. When I was eight, we had a water diviner, (dowser), to locate a water supply. I had tried to copy him, and found that I could also locate under ground springs. I cut a forked stick from the hedge, and set to work. I was able to mark a line across the fields where I thought the pipe ran. Others were, to say the least, sceptical. However, for want of a better idea, they started digging. The pipe was, to my relief found quite easily, only a few inches from my line. At the first hole, they found a stop tap, long since forgotten, so we set to work on rusty pipes with wrenches and spanners. We removed the stop tap and out came a very smelly frog's leg, followed by a good flow of water. We replaced the tap and went to see if we had water in the house. To our relief, all was flowing as it should be. We did not tell Mum and Gran about the frog's leg, we just said there had been a blockage!

It was sometime after this that a neighbour, Freddie, who had heard of our adventures with the water pipe, asked if I would use my divining skills to locate a place to dig a new well. This frightened me somewhat, just looking for a pipe, was a good deal different from finding a place, somewhere on his ninety acres, to dig a well. At first I refused, but he said that there would be no recriminations if I failed. So, at thirteen years old, I started walking over Fred's farm with my little forked stick. To Fred's credit, he didn't follow me around. I spent two days walking up and down, and round and round. There were two places that seemed to send my stick twitching, one at the top of the hill, one at the bottom. I thought that they were both from the same spring, the one at the bottom of the hill being further along. After much pacing, round the location, I decided that the spring was about thirty feet down. This based on a circular sounding that I had seen done previously. Fred employed an ex miner to dig the well, there were lots in the Forest of Dean. I must admit, I kept well away. We all heard about the progress via the local grapevine! After a couple of weeks, we heard that the well was thirty feet deep and there was no sign of water. I felt awful, but Fred said that it had been worth it, because if water was found so high on the hill, it would have flowed by gravity and would have been a cheap source. It was some weeks later, that Fred had been passing the hole, looked in and seen that it was full to within three feet of the top. He came across to us to give us the good news, and we all went to inspect. We moved from the area two years later and the water supply had not let Fred down. However, the whole process worried me so much that I have not dowsed for anyone since!

Dad and me, Whitmore Farm

Whitmore Farm, Longhope

View of May hill, from Whitmore Farm

Mowing circa 1955

Chapter Three

Daisy's Hen Party!

This area of the Forest of Dean was, at that time, renowned for the production of fruit for making cider. Indeed, our farm had cider apple and pear trees in every field. These trees grew to immense heights and produced hundredweights of fruit. We were new to this bountiful harvest, as were our cows. We knew that the fruit was almost ready for picking, and had arranged to start picking on the next dry day, as the brewers only took dry fruit. Unfortunately for us, we had a gale in the night and most of the apples and pears were blown off. One might think that this would solve the picking problem and so it did. The trouble was that the cows were in the same fields as the fruit. Cows are rather partial to fruit, but unfortunately, they don't know when to stop, a bit like us I suppose! When we went to get the cows in for milking, we were greeted by a very sorry looking herd. Cows have a large stomach, called a rumen, and this is designed as a fermentation tank to break down proteins. If they fill this tank with say, cider apples, they ferment. Fermenting cider apples produce cider.

Now I should think Daisy and her friends had each eaten about a hundredweight of apples, which would have produced several gallons of very rough cider. I have been on the receiving end of too much cider, and I did feel sorry for them. Also a bit worried, as too much fermentation could kill them. Daisy was leaning against a tree, moaning gently, her eyes rolling. Several of her wayward pals were laying down making long low groans, and others were still trying to pack in a few more apples, even though they could barely stand.

I made them all get up; there were many protests as I tried to get them moving to the yard. They looked a bit like Napoleon's relief of Mafeking. They couldn't walk in a straight line; in fact some could barely walk at all! They staggered from side to side, tripping over any obstacle, however small. It took me nearly an hour to move them a few hundred yards, every time I moved one on, the others all stopped, looking at me with their eyes crossed, and dribble running from the corner of their chops. On arrival in the yard, they stood against anything that would hold them up, some were leaning against the walls, and some were leaning against each other. They looked a sorry sight! We tried to milk them, but they were not very obliging at all, and our production that day was half the normal amount. We kept them in for the rest of that day and the following night to let them sober up.

Cows are also rather partial to plums. We had some Blaisdon plum trees in the corner of a field, and several cows visited this area regularly in the season to enjoy any fallen fruit. These usually fell in quite small numbers, so they couldn't over indulge. We had one cow that used to stand up on her back legs to reach the ripening fruit and she had to be watched for over indulgence. When cows eat plums, they regurgitate the plum stones when they chew the cud. It was not uncommon, while milking, to hear the stones rattling and ricocheting off the concrete walls and manger, as they spat them out!

It was usual in the locality, after sending cider fruit to the brewers, to receive a forty gallon barrel of cider back in return. We certainly did not want to upset anyone by refusing such an offer, so we gladly accepted and the barrel duly arrived. Now I am sure that everyone has heard of "rough cider", but this was rough in the extreme. We were told that it would mature, and would be better as time went on. Strangely enough, even though we found it positively revolting at first, we gradually became accustomed to it. The more consumed, the better it tasted! Stories were circulated amongst the locals, that the brewery always included a dead rat in every barrel. I am not sure about this, whether they found a dead rat and inserted it into the barrel, or whether a live one was used. If the latter, one can assume the rat died a happy little chap! My Grandfather who stayed with us on occasions, asked about the barrel and as he was strictly teetotal, we said it was just apple juice, which it was, so he said he would like to try some. I am pleased to say he did not enjoy it at all and I think that his wife, who was even more strictly teetotal, had a few quiet words with him.

Some years later, I had an encounter with cider, which still haunts me to this day. We had been working exceedingly hard loading and stacking bales of hay. It was lunch time, the cowman at that time, arrived with three bottles of cider. Quart bottles! We were very thirsty, and it was very hot and we had been perspiring profusely. The cider went down like water. It was midday, we should stop for lunch, but we started a competition to see who could throw off the most bales. The whole thing became a riot of laughter and jollity. As it was practice in hot weather on the farm, to work only in shorts, this was all we were dressed in. We were also wearing our wellies, as we supposed to be getting the cows in for milking. We had a much better idea, lets go for a swim, the beach was very near. This we did and as we walked, or possibly staggered across the well populated beach, could not understand why we were attracting so much attention. What the hell! Who cares? We certainly didn't. We ran into the lovely cooling water, and attempted to swim. If anyone else has tried to swim in wellies, they will realise the difficulty we had. It was now quite obvious why we had been receiving quizzical looks. Very few people try swimming in wellies, and I know the reason why. Half a gallon of salt water is surprisingly sobering, and we were back out quite quickly. We squelched sheepishly back across the beach and made for home amid derisive cheers from laughing bystanders. Never under estimate the power of cider!

There were many fruit trees on the farm, and we had a dedicated orchard of five acres. This contained both eating and cooking apples. The eating apples were delicious and I always took one or two to school with me for my lunch. My friends started to ask if I could take them one as well, which I did. After a while, I was taking six or seven apples with me every day, so I decided that I would make a small charge of two pence per apple. My business was thriving quite nicely, but as I have found throughout life, someone else wants to out do your efforts. Others started doing the same, at a penny per apple, so I had to bring my price down as well. Well, a penny is better than nothing, but, Dad had realised what I was doing, and started to charge me a penny an apple. So that was a sharp lesson in business. I ceased trading.

We transported our apple, pear and plum produce to Gloucester market with afore mentioned Morris 10cwt Light van. These excursions were not without mishap. We had by this time had a new clutch fitted, so it was now, no longer necessary, to reverse up steep inclines. This was long before the days of M.O.T's, and traffic speeds were very much more sedate than today. We could load many crates of apples aboard, and the more there was, the lower the transport cost. That old van struggled her way to market, coughing and spluttering at every corner and incline. This went on for some time and we all became accustomed to the protests. The problem arose, when we could not sell the fruit one week, and had to bring them back home. As I have said, the road to the farm was exceedingly steep, one in three. This caused little problem going with a full load, as it was downhill. However, coming home with a full load caused the old girl some serious problems. I am sorry to say, she expired half way up the drive and finished the trip being towed with the tractor. We never used our Morris 10cwt Light van again. It sat in the yard and housed a broody hen, who eventually hatched ten chicks.

<u>Woolly Jumpers!</u>

As May approached, there was some excitement generated amongst us all, sheep shearing, was the reason. We had not kept sheep before, and had no idea what to expect. To assist with shearing, sheep are kept indoors the night before. This has two reasons, one is that the sheep will be dry, wet sheep can't be shorn, the second reason, is to let the sheep become very warm. This warmth allows the lanolin at the base of the fleece to soften, thus allowing clippers to glide easily.

The sheep we were dealing with were forest sheep and as such were quite active. They had other ideas about being caught. We had them enclosed in a tight pen, but even then there were sheep that appeared to be crossed with kangaroos! I had the somewhat tedious task of catching and taking them to the shearers. When starting in the morning, one has this air of optimism that it will be O.K. So off you go like a bull in a china shop, trying to catch a sheep. The trouble is, the sheep have had a lovely restful night as well, and they are well refreshed. As one approaches, even though the pen is not large, the sheep seem to be able to compact themselves into a smaller and smaller space. This allowed them to dodge my first attempts. The two shearers could see my predicament, and were somewhat amused, and started making, what I shall now refer to as derisory comments. They are better not repeated at this time! However, I did catch the first sheep and dragged the reluctant animal to a shearer; there were a few more ribald comments. The next animal saw how I had caught the first one, and decided that she would take evasive action, the evasive action she chose, was to pass between my slightly open legs at great speed. Now I had my wellingtons on, sheep pens do become a little soiled after a while and also extremely slippery. A sheep travelling as fast as it is able, passing between slightly open legs, has rather a devastating effect, legs being forced outwards on slippery concrete continue going outwards, and two things happen. You do the splits, and fall backwards, both are extremely painful and when you arise, you appear to have cleaned most of the pen with your clothes! I hobbled about mentioning words that a thirteen year old shouldn't, but it hurt! Others were by this time rolling about as well, though not, I might say, in pain. Once again, I was receiving uncomplimentary comments, entirely undeserved. My body and pride were hurting, but I had to put on a brave face and carry on. I eyed up another ewe, she appeared to have a wry smile on her face. Perhaps she would be more obliging. Arms outstretched, LEGS TOGETHER, I approached. The ewe just stood looking at me, ah! I thought, she knows when she's met her match, but, just as I was about to grab her by her woolly fleece, she made a mighty jump, and went over my shoulders.

My attempts at catching sheep improved as the day wore on. It was an extremely hot day, catching hot sheep, dragging them to where they don't want to go, and the muck and grease all took a toll on sapping my strength and by the time we finished for the day, I was, to put it mildly, bushed. We had eaten and drunk on the move, as it were, no one wants to stop. By the days end one has an air of sheep about ones person, that flies appear to relish. It was usual to remove all clothing before going into the house. I remember dragging off my trousers and actually standing them up on their own! So much lanolin and muck had been absorbed.

The Latchen Room

Life was not all hard work, although I used to enjoy being on the farm, and learning new skills. This I found appealed to me much more than school. But, I had some good friends, and we went to the pictures once a week in the Village Hall, which for some unknown reason was called the Latchen Rooms. The films were certainly not the latest releases, by any means, but they made a social occasion. Monday nights, six thirty we trouped in. The highlight of these evenings was, of course, when the film broke and we were all left sitting in the dark until it was mended. I lived about two miles from the venue, so I had to set off at quarter to six. The shortest route was across five fields and then half a mile on the road. This was my route on many occasions. I don't ever remember using the longer route on the road. On the way, as my route joined the main road, I would be accompanied by my friend Vivienne. She was a happy girl, and we had some very pleasant journeys along that half mile stretch of road. Sometimes, she would stay with me across some of my otherwise, lonely walk across the fields. When we came to the final steep fields, she would return and I could watch her as she went back. Strangely enough, I do not remember any evenings when it was raining. I only remember the moon, a few clouds, and magnificent starry nights. Young eyes could see well in the moonlight and I could sit on the stile and watch Vivienne return back to the road. I remember these times with great affection, as it was really the only time that I was alone with a female. These were good times, and we made the most of them!

There were other activities at the Latchen Room, the annual show was a must, and I would enter whatever we had available at the time. It may be apples, pears, plums, or even a collection of wild flowers. It was with the latter that I took first prize one year, memory is a little hazy, but possibly I was the only entry! Looking back now, this was a time that gave me extreme pleasure, with all the new feelings and excitement of a teenager. These few experiences were the last really memorable ones of my early years. Things were to change rapidly.

Chapter Four

A Little History

Michael Burnett Hatton was born on Friday 10th February 1939 in Bournemouth, that's me! My brother Thomas Christopher Hatton was three years and ten months older than I. At four years old, I wanted to go to school so badly that I went with my brother to a small private school a few hundred yards away from where we lived. The first day, I didn't stop crying. After that I was fine. It was war time; Dad had joined the army when I was nine months old, and so I didn't remember him at all. Having said that, as we had no bonding with him, meant that we didn't really miss him. We were aware that times were not good, with rationing and shortages, but we knew no different, so we were happy. Yes, we queued at the grocers, the butchers, the fish shop and the bakers, but this was normal to us. We had the countryside adjoining the garden where we lived in Kinson, and within minutes we could be running across green fields or skinny dipping in the river close by. They were innocent times that we all enjoyed and the sun always shone. That last statement can't be true, but it seems that way. After I had been at my first school for about six months, the teacher, there was only one and she taught in her lounge, decided that she didn't want to teach any more. Whether this was anything to do with me I don't know! Mum looked around and found a private school in Winton, about four miles or so from Kinson. My brother and I presented ourselves and I was extremely happy there, for eighteen months when they also decided that they'd had enough of teaching. Could it be me? Looking back I do wonder whether it was me, but I didn't think of that at the time. Now there was no option, I would have to attend Kinson Primary School. Possibly this was because the money that she was receiving from Dad's service pay would not stretch to feeding a growing family. This was much closer and I could walk the mile or so each way. The school didn't have a canteen, so I had to come home at midday. The private schools had been extremely small by comparison to Kinson. They had only thirty or so pupils, Kinson had five hundred and a very strict Head Mistress, Miss Ward. I enjoyed this period, as I had become more used to making friends and did join in with their games. My school work was excellent at this time and I was selected as head of my form. I loved writing poetry and stories and several of these were copied into my form teacher's book in my best hand writing! She was a young teacher, though children don't always try to age people, I would think that Miss Breton was in her early twenties and very attractive and well endowed. Even an eight year old noticed that! At eight years old, we were destined to move again and I attended my fourth school at Three Legged Cross C of E School.

As you may have realised from my ramblings so far, we were certainly not by any stretch of the imagination, affluent farmers. Quite the reverse was true. During World War Two, farming was extremely remunerative. Dad had spent most of the war years in Burma, and on his demob, he swore that neither of his two sons would ever have to face the terrible conditions and trauma that he had to endure in that hellhole. He left the British Army with a demob suit and four hundred pounds. I was only six when he came home; I was taken from my bed at half past ten at night and told that this man was my Dad. I was only nine months old when he enlisted, so, to me he was a stranger. It was the same for many of my friends and we accepted things as they were and carried on regardless! At the time, of course, I didn't realise how difficult it would have been for him. He had missed out on my first six years, and this is a time of "bonding". We were strangers. It wasn't for another six or seven years that we really got to know each other.

Dad's idea was to purchase some moor land at Three Legged Cross, about seven miles from where we lived in Kinson, near Bournemouth. This land was covered in heather and gorse, with a sprinkling of stunted fir trees. He didn't have sufficient funds with his Army gratuity, so he used all the money Mum had saved, and any more that was available. Eventually he had enough cash to purchase twelve acres of this land. He had no cash left to work the land, but the government wanted food and the land would be ploughed and cultivated by what was called The War Ag. (War Agricultural Department). This, in due course, happened and I'm sure that there would have been much anxiety, both from Dad, and Mum. At six one tends to accept things as normal!

A good crop for cleaning land and helping to increase fertility is potatoes. So, Dad, Chris, who was four years my senior, and I, now seven, spent our Easter holidays planting potatoes in this rough and in some places, boggy land. I suppose, the War Ag., supplied the fertiliser and seed, I didn't ask, I just kept on planting. If anyone has planted ten acres of potatoes by hand, they will know the discomfort that has to be endured.

Amazingly, the crop yielded quite well and then, of course, there is lifting potatoes. Now, planting is back aching, but you cover the ground quite quickly and at least you can see what you've done fairly soon. Lifting potatoes is a different story. You grovel in the soil, trying not to leave any of the precious crop behind. After filling your container, it has to be taken to the nearest sack and tipped in. I'ts slow and extremely arduous work. As it was five miles back home, the three of us slept at night in a shelter that Dad had made from dipping old sacks in a cement and water mix and nailing them to a wooden frame. Surprisingly, this shelter was quite warm and dry and anyway, we were so tired that we could've slept on the clothes line!

Looking back now, it would be reasonable to assume that this crop would have increased the availability of cash, but I suppose that most of the income went to pay back the War Ag for the ploughing and potato seed purchase. Things did improve a little, Dad purchased ten goats. He also purchased a concrete block making machine. A simple piece of equipment that allowed him to make about thirty blocks a day. A wooden pallet, nine inches by eighteen inches, was placed in a rectangular box at the rear of the machine, the size of a nine inch thick concrete block. This was filled with concrete, (mixed by hand). A heavy weight on a lever was banged down several times, pressure on a foot pedal raised the block so that it could be carefully carried away and left to dry. Another pallet was placed in the machine and the process repeated. This machine was used to make blocks for several years and we built a store shed, a goat house and a long wall to join the buildings together and make a cattle yard. Really, the only limitations were the pallets available, and the ability to mix lots of concrete!

The store shed was the first to be built, and during the summer holidays, I spent many nights sleeping there. There was no electricity or mains water, no telephone or drainage. The Primus stove was our kettle boiler and was used to cook anything that needed it. Actually, we didn't cook much, but we did heat up lots of baked beans. We went to bed fairly early, as we were very tired after a days work. I'm sure that, after our baked bean supper, the shed was rather unpleasant to the casual visitor. If we needed a light in the evening, we had a hurricane lamp. Strangely, I remember these times quite affectionately and I was blissfully happy working with Dad and preferred it to school. I was seven years old at this time, going on eight. To get from Kinson to Three Cross, was a bus journey, where I had to change busses near Ferndown. I made this trip on my own on most occasions and became quite well known with the bus conductors. It's a sign of the times, but I wouldn't want one of my Grandchildren attempting that journey on their own today!

Dad had also made a fire and boiler arrangement for boiling potatoes for the chicken. My friend (who was five years older than I) were asked by Dad to light this one day. We were both amateurs and after three attempts, we still had no fire. "I know" Said my friend, "let's put some petrol in the hearth, that'll get it going," he splashed some petrol into the fire, and I bent down in front to light it. Big mistake. There was quite an explosion and I was blown backwards on the ground. My hair was singed, I had no eyebrows, my arms and face were burning hot. My friend was in a similar condition. It took several weeks before the burns had healed. I had great respect for petrol from that day on.

We also constructed, about this time, a large galvanised iron shed to house poultry. We now had eggs to sell and goats milk to sell. Eggs were sold locally and found a ready market. A cash source at last! The goat's milk was collected by a firm and distributed in the larger towns. Things were beginning to look up a bit and the land was now productive, but by no means fertile, Dad was able to raise a mortgage and we had a bungalow built near the entrance, beside the stream where we had been getting our water supply. The bungalow was slow to be built, it was just after the second world war and wood, bricks and tiles were all in short supply. It was eventually completed and with great excitement, we moved from Kinson, where we had shared a house with Mum's mother and father. Transport was also difficult at this time and the only vehicle Dad could find was the coal man! So, all of our furniture, bicycles and chattels, were piled high on the coal lorry. I still have this mental picture of this vehicle, piled high and on the very top, was the cat box with our two pet cats. I can't imagine that they enjoyed their journey very much, but they didn't seem to bear any grudges and were just as friendly when they were released at their destination.

Life now became much easier, no more travelling. I had to start a new school, but I had already attended three different ones, so I wasn't too worried and as we had been in the area for about eighteen months, I had got to know some of my new classmates.

We now had a well, a bathroom, a toilet, and we could pump water up into a tank in the roof to supply our needs. We still had to rely on paraffin light and a paraffin cooker, but things had certainly improved. It was just after we had moved in, when we noticed that the water from the well had a strange taste. We decided that we would only drink the water if it had been boiled. A wise precaution! Dad had a man from the water board, who he knew, to test the water, it failed the test and the sample contained sewage. What now? The builders who had put in the well came back, but they couldn't find a reason. The water board man returned with someone who could trace underground springs with a forked stick. I watched with interest and thought that I would try this out. Amazingly I found that I could find all the springs and pipes on our land. It was at this time that I was, there and then, offered a position when I left school as a water diviner for the water board. This was something that I never followed up, I wonder how different life would have been had I done so?

It was very obvious why we had polluted water, the spring that fed the well, ran past the septic tank first, contaminating the water. It was a major problem, and the builders that had put in the septic tank, had no inclination to move it. We did overcome it, but it took lots of concrete, lots of digging, and lots of swearing!

This, for me, was a happy time. The school was a small C of E school, with twenty or so pupils, ranging in age from five to eleven. I suppose, this was the first time we had all been together as a family and I enjoyed this immensely. The school had an outside toilet, consisting of a tin shed, with a trough leading to a bucket for the boys. I never ventured into the girls side, so what they used I have no idea. The shed was about six or seven feet high and I well remember that one of the older boys was able to pee over the roof. This was a talent that was well respected and no one else ever came close. This was not for want of trying!

I passed the eleven plus at this school, the only one to do so in very many years. So now I was off to Wimborne Grammar School. I was alone again; all of my friends went to the secondary school. I wore quite thick spectacles; I had inherited a sight problem from Mum. On the first day at Wimborne, I was nicknamed Nelson and that stuck until I left nine months later.

My reason for leaving was that Dad had decided that it was time to move to a larger farm, as Chris was fifteen, and about to leave school. This meant that it would need more than these few acres for the two of them. After much negotiating and many farm visits, it was decided to sell Three Cross land as a small holding, and purchase twenty eight acres in Nailsworth, Gloucestershire.

This time a friend, who owned a van, relocated us. He took furniture and various odds and ends, but Dad had sold the holding "lock stock and barrel". This meant that all stock and equipment were included in the sale. This suited us quite well, as it meant that we did not have transport costs for this, quite long distance.

We arrived at our new farm at the end of a beautiful day, although it had been very hot in the car we had travelled in. As a moving present, (possibly glad to see us go)! An Aunt took us all from Three Cross to Nailsworth in their Alvis shooting brake that they used in their hotel business.
It was at this time that I started school in Stroud.

The school that I attended was Marling School, Stroud. I made some good friends there, unfortunately I did not keep in contact with them, but when we moved on we tended to loose touch with people.

Because of my thick spectacles and my short sightedness, I was excused rugby, but I still had to put on my kit and run the line. Our sports master had been an army P.T. instructor, so stood no nonsense from little boys. We only wore shorts, we had bare feet and the floor was very cold in winter. At the first sign of misbehaviour, he would line up the culprits, tell them to remove their shorts and bend over. He then walked along the line with a gym shoe administering a wallop on each bottom as he passed.

Rough justice, but it worked, and I think everybody liked him.

I had problems with the French teacher. French was not a strong point with me and I never could get the hang of those verbs. By the end of the lesson Mr Tom Watson would be screaming at me, "I'll bump you boy, you think you're the cat's pyjamas, but you're not" which I took to heart, as I had never ever given a thought as to being the cat's or anyone else's pyjamas and the more he shouted the more flustered I became and I usually ended up in tears. During the lesson he had seen fit to throw chalk, blackboard cleaner and any other object he could lay his hands on.

In the next door classroom was our English teacher. He would say quietly to me, "Bit of a rough afternoon, Hatton?" He could hear everything through the thin classroom walls. This small remark was sufficient to reassure me and I knew he was sympathetic towards me. He was a good teacher and I enjoyed English and did quite well at it.

I learnt so much, practically, by working on the farm and possibly this meant I didn't learn academically. During the two years or so at Fooks Farm, I learnt to start and drive tractors, carry out basic plumbing, electrical wiring, hedge-laying, stone walling, milking, calving cows and possibly other life skills that have become second nature to me, but I did not learn French! I still remember the countryside and particularly the farm with warm affection.

My first home,
The Glen, Kinson

Chris and me

Dad at Fooks Farm,
Nailsworth

Chapter Five

End of Term

By the time I was fifteen, my school work was not of a very high standard, possibly because of my having attended seven different schools, I had lost interest, and the inclination to learn about things that were of little interest to me. It was possible to leave the Grammar school at fifteen, although the correct leaving age was sixteen. Dad had to write a letter to the Headmaster, giving good reasons for me to leave. He knew I was not happy there, and this he agreed to do. The Headmasters comments were that he thought education was as important in farming as in all other walks of life. However, he must have looked at my reports and decided that he would be able to manage without me! Looking back now, I suppose I wasn't that bad at school, my position in the form never went below twentieth out of thirty two, and I was always in the A form.

With an extra full time helper, we decided that we could increase our income by growing vegetables and selling them either in the village shop, or if a surplus, Gloucester Market. Consequently, an area was ploughed and tilled ready to receive the carrot, lettuce, leek and swede seed. We raked the area by hand, to remove all greenery and surface rubbish and then laboriously marked out the drill rows and then the seed was sown and we raked over the area again. The work was long and back aching, even for a youngster like me, what it did to Dad, I cannot recall. We watched and waited, the area was soon a mass of green as every weed imaginable decided that, having been buried for many years, now was their chance! We spent every daylight hour on our hands and knees, picking out weeds. This was the only way it could be done, as weeds and seedlings were of a similar height and colour. It was extremely frustrating, as the weeds grew larger, the job took longer, as the job took longer the weeds grew bigger. Chris, at this time, decided to join the local cricket team and it was a great shame that he was so good at it. The better he became at cricket, the more he had to practice. There was a game every Saturday, one Wednesday evening and practices most evenings. To me, it was beyond a joke and I had a little rebellion. It didn't last long; I could never hold a grudge for very long. Dad, Mum and I worked our socks off trying to keep on top of the weeding, but it was really a case of fighting a loosing battle! The rows we cleared exposed lovely vegetable plants. We had on the farm, lots and lots of rabbits. They love vegetables that are nicely exposed. When we came back in the morning, the vegetables had gone. It was all a great waste of time and, more importantly, money. Although, money may be the root of all evil, I am afraid without it, one is up a creek without a paddle! It was at about this time that we lost our second paddle and we could not travel very far. The farm was mortgaged, but we were not getting sufficient income from our cows to keep the family. We had a bad year, the calves that were born did not survive and the grass did not grow well, so the cows did not yield well, so our funds were in a negative state. Things became desperate; no funds were available to us. However there would be some funds available if we sold the farm. Looking at the price of farms in Devon, it would be possible to buy a much larger farm and still have the same mortgage, as land was much cheaper in Devon than in Gloucester at this time.

So, it came to pass that Dad and Chris went to Devon to inspect some likely properties. Mum, Gran and I remained; someone had to do the work! we were hand milking eighteen cows. Chris mostly did the milking, except when cricketing, then Dad and I worked our way through it. Hand milking is the sort of job that the more you do, the faster you are. I was still quite slow, usually milking only about four cows to Chris's fourteen. This was partly because I did the awkward ones that fidgeted or were at the end of their lactation.

As they left on the bus to go to Gloucester station, I was given various instructions. The milk churns had to be on the churn stand at the end of the drive for midday; it was at this time that the lorry collected our milk. Oh! And be careful driving the tractor down the drive. There was sufficient food for the two days that they would be away, left available for me to give the cows. Dad and Chris waved goodbye at two o'clock in the afternoon. Now it was up to me. I felt a bit apprehensive, but if I had real difficulty, our neighbour Fred was lined up to assist.

I fed the cows early that afternoon, so that I could get a good start with the milking, we usually milked at five in the afternoon, and I decided that would start at four. Cows are funny creatures, they get used to a particular milker, and get quite upset if someone different tries to massage their personal parts. My usual girls were quite happy, but the others did some aggressive protesting, a cow protests by offering you her foot at a very generous speed and on a generous number of occasions! There were feet, muck, curses and oaths flying in all directions. At this point Mum came in and asked innocently,

"Everything alright"? I still regret my answer to this day, but Mums are very forgiving! Milking usually took about two hours, finishing at about seven o'clock. I finished at half past ten, six and a half hours and the milk yield was down by thirty per cent. I went in after giving the cows their last feed of hay, a very tired and grumpy bunny!

Now just because you have milked the cows now, doesn't mean the end of the job, oh no! I knew that I would have the same process again in the morning. I set the alarm for four am. So that I should be finished for ten. What a joke! Because the cows had held back some of their milk the previous evening, they now decided that I could have it this morning. The first ones were not too bad, as I was two hours earlier than normal. As I worked my way doggedly through, I was getting later and later. The later I became, the more milk each cow gave. It was eleven thirty when I tipped in the last pail of milk. I asked Mum to feed the cows, and set about starting the tractor. This was a Fordson Major, quite a high beast; I turned on the petrol, pushed in the choke, and pulled up on the starting handle. After four pulls, she sprang into life with a roar. What a relief!

We had four or five churns that weighed about thirty five pounds each when empty, each churn holding about ten gallons of milk weighing about one hundred pounds, a total weight of approximately one hundred and thirty pounds each. These, I now had to lift onto the trailer. I managed this, I must admit, not without some difficulty and then slowly set off down the drive. It was now after mid-day, but I dare not go fast down the one in three drive way. I arrived at the churn stand only to find a note from the lorry driver saying that he couldn't wait. I admit now, that I called everyone I could think of some very objectionable names! I stood at the roadside, wondering what to do, should I drive after him and see if I could catch him at another farm? I had no licence to drive on the roads, but that wasn't a reason to stop me. I had just seated myself on the tractor, when neighbour Fred arrived, he had seen me coming down the drive, and as the milk lorry driver was at his place, he had asked him to call back to me. I could have kissed him, but I refrained, it may be misconstrued in this agricultural area, I certainly did not want to start rumours!

Dad and Chris returned later on the next day, "Every thing O.K"? They asked, "Fine" I replied. But you and I now know differently, don't we? It was a great responsibility to give a fifteen year old lad, but I suppose that they must have known that I would manage. This was the first of three occasions when I was left to run the farm and each time it was a similar experience.

The Find

The farm that Dad and Chris had looked at on their third trip appeared suitable. Yes, there were several drawbacks, but very little is perfect! The farm was 182 acres, dairy and arable, with a cob and thatch house and outbuildings. Cob was a mixture of mud and stones, and as long as the rain was kept off, it lasted for many years. The outbuildings had galvanised iron roofs, that were very rusty, "Nothing that a coat of tar won't cure", said Chris, he was always an optimist, his best and most frequent saying was, "What can go wrong"? We usually found out quite quickly! I didn't see our new farm at all until we moved in, come to think of it, neither did Mum. Usually, moves to new accommodation have to be undertaken with the full and positive agreement of the feminine part in a relationship, but Mum had no input whatsoever. She was extremely long suffering.

Our move to Devon was not without incident. The cattle were sold; it would be cheaper to replace them at Devon's market price. Our furniture was again loaded on a cattle truck. The smaller bits and pieces were put into a trailer I had made from the chassis of the Morris 10 cwt. Light van! It was a smallish two wheel affair, and I used what I could find on the farm. The drawbar was from a disused mower and the sides and base were made from the boards of an old chicken shed. When it was all painted, it looked quite smart. The vehicle that was to be used to tow the trailer was a Standard twenty that was at the end of its days. It was another of Dad and Chris's purchases that, shall we say, were not very prudent. Certainly it was cheap; I think it was twenty five pounds. On their way home they ran out of petrol, on inspecting the petrol filler cap, it was found to be wired closed and the wire was rusty, so obviously it wasn't the usual way to fill with fuel. They opened the boot and found a five gallon can inside, with a piece of rubber tubing coming out of the top and disappearing through the boot floor, supposedly to the engine. So this was the petrol tank. They had some fuel put into the can, and after much cranking of the engine, it started and they soon arrived back home. We hadn't had a saloon car before and I must admit the vehicle did look quite impressive. We really didn't want the boot full of petrol can, as there was little room for anything else, so we tackled that problem as soon as we were able. It became obvious why the tank filler had been wired up; any petrol inserted in the top, very swiftly came out the bottom! After much grovelling beneath the vehicle, we emerged with the petrol tank. I use the term petrol tank, in its loosest form, no way would this rusty metal hold petrol. Chris, still being optimistic, went to the local garage to see if any product was available that could be used to patch the bottom of the tank. He returned with some fibrous layers of material, and a resin that the garage owner had assured would seal anything. I must admit I was sceptical, but he had bought the stuff, so we may as well give it a try. Chris went to milk the cows and I was left to work miracles. It was a tedious job, sanding the base of the tank, every time I rubbed an area, more holes appeared. It took hours and I finally covered the whole of the tank base with the resin. It was left to set overnight, and on inspection the following morning, looked to have made a good seal. We poured a small amount of petrol into the tank and waited with baited breath. There was certainly a vast improvement, but there were still a couple of small leaks. This was looking hopeful, so we set about the offending area with renewed vigour. Amazingly, we sealed that petrol tank, and it lasted for the rest of the vehicles life. There were several other matters that were a bit of a problem with the car, but it had a drawbar, and could pull my trailer. We had a trial run up and down the drive a few times, and decided that if it could take that, it would be alright for the trip to Devon.

The Move

On the moving day, we all started early, the furniture had been loaded the night before. Chris set off in the lorry to show the driver the way, as he had been there twice. Dad, Mum, Gran, Judy (my dog) and I, set off after loading all the remaining bits and pieces into the trailer. The trailer had solid sides, about five feet high and it was covered with a tarpaulin. We filled it to the top and the last two items were our two cats.

The distance between Gloucester and Devon, was about two hundred miles, this included Devon lanes, but excluded any motorway, as this had still to be invented. We calculated that at thirty miles an hour, we should do the trip in seven hours. Notice the adjective, should. At Bristol, we took a wrong turn and ended up thirty miles off course. While we were making this detour, we had a puncture in the near side rear tyre. Our spare wheel and jack and wheel brace were in the trailer, quite well hidden. We had to remove them without releasing two very puzzled pussies into the countryside. We managed this and started to undo the nuts to remove the offending wheel. We removed the first two, but the other two had no intention of shifting. It was a very long time ago that these were last removed. After much jumping up and down on the wheel brace and using every item we had with us, we were finally beaten. We didn't at this time belong to the A.A. but we were now about to join. I walked about a mile or so to a lonely farm and luckily, they had a phone. At that time many properties were not connected to the telephone and it was a bit hit and miss. The A.A. were summoned and duly arrived. We had now lost over two hours of our precious timetable. We were persuaded to join the A.A. I don't think the gentleman would have been so helpful if we hadn't.

Eventually we moved off again, but I am sorry to relate that we had the same occurrence on one more occasion. This was somewhere on the A39, I neither knew nor cared where, by this time we were all very much past caring. We had stopped on several occasions to eat our prepared food, and have a drink. For toilet stops, we always found a convenient hedge, but Gran had suffered from having a stroke recently and couldn't manoeuvre as well as we could. I still remember, as we drove nonchalantly away from a lay-by, the long stream of water that stretched from the car door, to the other end of said lay-by.

It was past eleven o'clock at night. We were looking for a specific turning off of the A39, it was very dark and most of the road junctions looked the same. Dad had been this way twice before, but not at night. He decided that it was this turn, so we set off; very slowly, as the lane was narrow with grass growing up the middle. At the next crossroads, we stopped to inspect a half hidden signpost, I alighted and went knee deep in a pond. "Oh! Good"! Dad said, "I remember that pond, it's straight on now". Others in our party thought this amusing, but I didn't feel very amused. At the next cross roads we saw a ford and this was the entrance to the farm.

As we approached the house, we expected to see Chris waiting anxiously, but everything was in darkness and no sign of anyone. There wouldn't have been a lot of light, as electricity had not reached this far into Devon. We blew the horn repeatedly, but nothing. We all piled stiffly out of the car and stumbled about in the dark. We had given Chris all the torches and lamps, as we would be there long before dark, we thought. We had no idea of the layout of the house; it had seven bedrooms, two large reception rooms, office and kitchen, so it was not easy to see where we were going, or even where we wanted to go! One good thing, the furniture was in the house, so he and it, had arrived safely, but where was he. Dad suggested that perhaps the previous owner had seen him here on his own and taken Chris back with him. We found first a candle, which enabled us to locate the Bi-Aladdin. This was a pressurised paraffin lamp that appeared, at that time extremely bright. We lit this and started to explore. Where was Chris? He will be worried to death, we thought. We found him, fast asleep, on a sofa in the office. "I was a bit tired and fed up waiting", he said grumpily. Me too, I thought.

We decided to leave the cats in the trailer and sort them out in the not too distant morning, but as Mum fed them, they decided they'd had enough, and disappeared into the blackness. They were still about the next morning and were none the worse for their adventure. The next day was exploration day, both indoors and outside. We had only had fifty acres at Longhope; we were now exploring one hundred and eighty two acres, with woodland, streams, pastures and arable. The buildings consisted of three long sheds, between seventy and eighty feet in length and perhaps fifteen feet wide. They were all made of cob, all with tin roofs. It was obvious that when these buildings were new, they'd had a thatch roof. All the sheds ran parallel to the house, which was also about seventy feet long. It looked very picturesque, but very drab and dreary. The house was thatched with local wheat straw, the walls made of cob. It had a really cosy feel to it when you were inside, and in fact was warm in the winter and kept cool in the summer.

We needed to receive an income as soon as possible, but there was nowhere suitable for milking cows. This was the first job and we soon had some standings built in one of the sheds so that we could tie up cows for milking. We then went to local sales and bought ten cows. These still had to be hand milked at this time. We had no electricity, a poor water supply, no telephone, but, glory of glories, we had a flush loo! The cistern was filled by rain water from the gutter, so if it didn't rain, you didn't flush! Where the water etc went after flushing was a mystery we never solved, but it disappeared and gave us no problems.

Cooling the milk was a major headache, the water supply was intermittent, all the water had to be pumped via a lead pipe of huge bore and a pump which was made entirely of lead. Lead was an extremely expensive commodity at this time and we were able to exchange the pipe and pump for a small motorised pump. This was good, but if the well is empty then there is no point in pumping! There were several occasions during those first few months when the milk didn't get cooled properly and was rejected by the dairies. We tried many different ways of cooling milk, standing churns in cold water was tried, but if you put ten gallons of hot milk into a tank of cool water, you get a tank of warm water and churns of warm milk! In the winter we could manage, vast amounts of rain fell and the well produced all the water that was needed.

During our first winter in Devon, we planned and worked to increase the capacity, to have more cows. It was a mild winter, no snow, lots and lots of rain. The thirty cows we now had, were able to stay out all winter and were milking well. However, this was not sufficient income to support us all and pay off the interest on our mortgage. We needed more cows, but we were at the limit for hand milking. We would need a milking machine. The first milking machines were designed to run with a small petrol engine, no electricity was required. We purchased some pipe and fitted it along the back of the cows' stalls. Connected the machine, and hey presto! We had a milking machine. We were elated; the cows however, did not seem to have the same enthusiasm for it. In fact, they were quite cross about it. They weren't too happy with the noise, but when we attempted to attach the units to their private parts, all hell was let loose. There were feet flying in all directions and for some reason, the rubber pipes and tubes always seem to wind themselves round these flailing feet. The nicely clean milking units become encased in muck; the cows then proceed to shake their legs and consequently the units, until they were reduced to their smallest possible element. It can take half an hour to find, clean and rebuild a unit that has been properly set about in this way.

With much perseverance and tenacity, not to mention, swearing, this first machine milking was over. We didn't have much milk though, what wasn't on the floor, walls, or ourselves, was still being retained by the reticent cows! It took several weeks before milking became more normal, although some of the stronger willed cows were able to keep up the fight for months. Two of them never did agree with this new fangled machine, and sadly we parted company.

Now we could increase cow numbers and we brought the numbers up to fifty, about the limit for this type of machine. We decided that during the following summer we would build a milking parlour. These parlours were just beginning to be made and seemed to be an answer. There were none in Devon or Cornwall that we could ascertain, so we went to Somerset and saw one working there. It appeared to be ideal. We would be able to milk a hundred cows or so with this equipment. The cows walked to the machine, in groups of four or six, when they were milked, they then walked out, and the next group came in. it all sounded very simple and easy, but, no doubt there would be many problems to overcome.

<u>Chapter six</u>
<u>Beware, Builders at Work!</u>

Between milkings we concreted the cow yard, built a milking parlour, built a dairy and plumbed in a water supply to the dairy and parlour. We also had to make the hay, and get the corn harvest in. The days were long and the work hard.

We arose at five and my first job was to bring in the cows. This was fine when the mornings are light, but there aren't many days when it is light at that time. Finding the girls and persuading them to get up and walk back for milking was quite tedious at times.

We had an arrangement with our builder's merchant to deliver five tons of sand and gravel to us at seven. We had a stock of cement in the shed and after bringing in the cows I would put the required amount of cement onto the gravel. Now the work really began! I would start to mix this enormous pile with a shovel. Twice dry, add water and then twice wet. I had usually mixed it once by breakfast time. After feeding, I would have Dad and Chris to help, so it was much easier. Our aim was to get the concrete mixed and laid by dinner time. As the summer progressed the yard was concreted. Footings were dug for parlour and dairy, filled with concrete and walls built. Things were now taking shape. It was at the end of this hot and tiring summer that the builder's merchant announced that he had a concrete mixer that we could borrow. Better late than never I suppose, but we had been to several farm sales to purchase a mixer, but they were a bit like gold dust at that time, every farm was expanding and houses were popping up like mushrooms! We thanked him warmly and said, "Yes please". We still had much to do. The milking parlour was installed in September and we were able to increase the herd to eighty cows.

During the winter when the concreting was over we decided that it would be nice to have electricity. Mains electricity wasn't available, so we had to buy a generator. We bought one at a sale of ex R.A.F. equipment. It was quite large, but had no engine. We had at the farm a diesel engine that worked the saw bench, so we decided to attach this to the generator base plate. We calculated many times, to find the optimum size for the driving pulleys and finally fitted these and attached the driving belts. We were elated beyond belief, as the attached light bulb glowed brilliantly. This elation was short lived, as the light bulb went out with a ping. We were sure we had calculated correctly, but it was obvious that we were generating too high voltage.

I perused my library book on electric generators. There was a section that I had not read. It appeared that we would need a voltage regulator. When generators are running with little or no load, the voltage increases and vice versa. A regulator was needed to counteract this. When the generator had been delivered, there had been a load of bits and pieces with it. We searched through the pile of wires and dials and we found the necessary piece of equipment. After we had attached the regulator, all went well.

Now we had electricity, all we had to do was wire the whole farm and more especially the house. Dad had said that if we had electricity indoors, we could have a television!!! None of us had ever seen a television and we were excited beyond belief at the thought. We bought yards and yards of cable of different calibre and switches and bulb holders and sockets all for me to install. I hadn't tried this before, but my maxim had always been, if you can read a book, you can do anything! Basically, this has been true and most things that I have attempted have worked out passably. Not good, but passable. This is one reason for the statement at the beginning of this book, that I think I am very lucky!

I set to work with great enthusiasm and soon had lights in the milking parlour and dairy. I wired the house next, the thought of television spurring me on. We had never had such bright lights in the house before and the harshness of the electric light seemed to change the feel of the rooms. Dad was sent off to buy a telly. He returned with a quality fourteen inch television. I think it cost seventy something pounds. This would have bought two cows in the market, but Dad said that we had earned it. But I did feel a few pangs of guilt!

The television was plugged in, the aerial attached and now with baited breath, we waited for it to warm up, this took about five minutes with valve machines. At last! We had a flickering picture that kept on running up and down the screen. It was unwatchable. Chris, in disgust, decided he may as well go and do the milking; we stayed and played with the knobs. We were about to switch the useless thing off, when Chris switched on the milking machine. What a change! The picture became clear and bright. We had to leave a motor of some sort running all the time the generator was on if we wanted to watch the television. The generator had to be started by starting handle, so Mum couldn't attempt this operation. She always said that as soon as all the men left the farm, the generator would stop. I must admit that this did occur on a great number of occasions.

Expansion, at a Cost!

As suggested, we continued to expand, building a covered yard and other outbuildings. Each time we could afford it, we purchased more milking cows. Our borrowing was quite high and the repayments meant that there were little or no funds available for any of life's little extras. The house as I have said was made of cob with a thatched roof. We had, about that time, two years of more or less continuous rain. The fields were under water and we were even trying to combine barley in November, when we had a week's frosty weather. At hay harvest the fields were like lakes. The grass was cut and there it stayed, it rained for days on end.

It was during the second of these wet times, that during an extreme gale, that most of the thatch was torn from the roof of our house. The water started to run down the walls of the upstairs bedrooms and we had to move to different rooms. As the walls absorbed the water, they started to dissolve before our eyes. As daylight arrived, we could see the damage. It was a sad and sorry sight. As the cob had softened, the weight of the roof beams and wet thatch had lowered the roof at one end of the house by several feet. The house would not be fit to inhabit for much longer. Dad had an estate agent friend that had been trying to persuade him to build a new house on the farm ever since we had moved to Devon and he said that he would lend him the capital to do this. Really, I suppose, Dad was now caught between a rock and a hard place. He contacted the agent, who informed him that he had already had plans drawn up for a farm house and that he would get things moving.

We were sent copies of the house plans and they were extremely good. We found a suitable location, a little way from the farm buildings and on a piece of land that was raised higher than the surrounding area. It was at this time that it stopped raining. The new house was started in April and went ahead in glorious sunshine throughout the summer. We had stopped trying to make hay, as we had two years of very poor quality feed that had cost so much to balance with concentrates, that we had made little or no profit during this time. The new house was finished in October and the day before the builders finished, we had another very stormy night and the whole of the old house started to crumble away.

When the builders arrived the next morning, they found that we had already moved in.

This, to us, who had lived in old farm houses for many years, was amazing. We had electricity already wired in, but still from a generator. The generator we were now using started itself when a light or piece of equipment was switched on. It took a minute or two to get to maximum output, but it was a great improvement. We were still using a pump from a well to supply water, we didn't have the telephone, but we had a bathroom and flush toilet. What more could we want?

The new house cost a lot of money that we had to borrow from Dads estate agent friend. But, the weather had settled and now we were getting enough rain and enough dry weather to allow normal farming activities to proceed. Cow's yields increased, calves grew well and the silage that we now made to replace the disastrous hay making seasons was well on the way.

We were still using the Standard twenty at this time, it was very difficult to start and very easy to stop! Most of the normal day to day needs were delivered to the door. The grocer called with a van, the baker, the butcher and a hardware van with paraffin, mantles, spades, shovels and forks were all delivered to the door. There wasn't a lot of need to go out. Mum did insist occasionally, that she must go to the village for a special item, so it was then a major effort to start the car. The most difficult times were when we had run out of petrol. Without this we couldn't get out to get some more! On one occasion, the car had an empty tank, but we had a small amount in a can. We knew that such a small amount would be lost in a twelve gallon petrol tank, so had to find another way to make it last for the four miles to the village. The car had no air filter, so we decided that if someone rode on the running board of the car and poured in the petrol every time the engine stopped firing, we might make it. I don't remember how it happened, but I seemed to be nominated to carry out this, what now appears to be, highly dangerous, manoeuvre. Obviously, I did survive and we came to within a hundred yards of the garage. Anyone trying this today, would be arrested very quickly, I imagine, so don't try this at home!

On another occasion, the car would not oblige us at all; it refused point blank to start. After towing the beast up and down the road on several occasions and not receiving the slightest hint that it would start, I lost my temper with it and smacked a very large turnip onto the air intake. The effect was a wonder to behold, the engine roared into life and sounded better than it had for many weeks previous. The old girl was very dilapidated and I think the manifold gaskets were in poor shape along with the rest of her. It was shortly after this that we purchased a replacement for the Standard. The replacement was a Wolseley 6/90. A very smart car, as used in the police series that was running at the time on the television!

The television was the only source of entertainment for me, although I spent nearly every waking hour outside, either working or making something. I really enjoyed using the comprehensive workshop that I had built up. Since coming to Devon, I had barely left the farm and had made no friends of my age. I did at times, resent this, but to forget, I used to work. When moving to a new area where no one is known to you, it is difficult to make friends, especially if you have left school. There was little or no social life at all. I think I had become a very boring young man! A neighbour who was in the Young Farmers club offered to take me one month, I gladly accepted, but waited in vain for him to pick me up, as I didn't have a driving licence at that time. I never heard from him again about going to the Y.F. club, so that was the end of that!

We had gas and electric welders in the workshop, grinders, metal saws and every thing that I needed to repair broken machinery. We also had wood working tools and I made a lathe for wood turning. I loved doing this, and spent most of my evenings in the workshop.

I was, by this time, well into my twenties, I think twenty four and I had never had a holiday of any kind. I had on occasions had a day in Exeter, or Barnstaple, but I had to work before going and be back for late afternoon. Chris was better at making friends than I and he met several young ladies and went out at weekends and evenings. This did make me a little grumpy and I suppose I appeared as a bit of a misery.

We had purchased an old Fordson tractor that had been left out in the field for five years. It wouldn't start; the pistons were stuck fast in the bores. I had a great deal of satisfaction from completely dismantling the engine and rebuilding it. I had great difficulty removing the pistons, but after soaking in paraffin for days, they came out quite cleanly. After the overhaul, we all waited with baited breath as I went to start it. The tractor started after four pulls of the starting handle, I felt very satisfied and drove it to the field to try ploughing. What a treat, up hills we sailed, although the top speed of these tractors was only seven miles an hour. It sounded and looked like a new tractor, as I had also repainted it in its original colours. I was delighted!

So by now, I had gained a great number of skills and I suppose that I was lucky to be allowed to attempt these things with no previous experience. There were many, "cock ups", but nothing too serious. My list of achievements went something like this: - Thatcher, tractor driver, electrician, plumber, hedge layer, milker, builder, concrete mixer, roofer, mechanic and wood turner. I didn't realise it at that time, but these skills have been of tremendous use to me throughout my working life. Jack of all trades, master of none, comes to mind.

To bring some extra cash in, it was generally agreed by Dad and Chris that I should go to other farms to cut and carry their silage for them. This was a very good idea, as very few farmers at that time, had such efficient silage making equipment. We had a head start on most of them. I wasn't very sure, but I knew that the extra income would be a great boost to us. I started with the next door farmer and things expanded very quickly. Before very long I was taking the silage equipment fifteen to twenty miles from home. I drove the tractor all day, cutting the grass and blowing it into trailers. I would then unhook the forage harvester and take the load to the silage clamp. When one does this, day after day, it is surprising how fast the manoeuvres can become. The fastest time I could manage from getting off the tractor seat to getting back on again after unhooking the harvester, was ten seconds. I was somewhat more agile in those days!

The contracting went well, and I made silage for many farms in the area. The main problem was to get the money off the farmers afterwards. Some were excellent, but some never did pay, there was always a complaint when Dad went to collect. Either the silage wasn't as good as they expected, or a gate post had been broken, or a gate damaged. None of these things were mentioned when we left the farm after silage making, we always asked if they were satisfied. I think that times were as bad for them as for us, but that is still no reason not to pay, we had to buy fuel and spare parts etc., so we were the loser. After saying this, we did make a profit, but not as much as we would have done if all had paid up promptly.

The Last Straw!

It was along now that the estate agent backing us said he would like to invest some more capital in another farm. As a farm adjoining ours was on the market, he decided to purchase it. He wanted us to run it with our present equipment and stock. If we hadn't been stretched pretty well to the limit already, this would have been fine, but as things were, we were working fifteen hours a day, seven days a week. The main trouble was that he really held the purse strings, our mortgage was held by him and if he wanted to purchase more land we had no say in it. If we had to employ someone, we would not be able to make an income that would maintain the repayments and support us. If we didn't employ, we wouldn't get the work done to a standard that would be adequate for farming and animal husbandry. We tried something in between, part time employment, but the quality of the available staff, for us, was very poor. Jobs were not done well and we had to do most of them again ourselves. This was a waste of time and money.

We started to realise that we had possibly bitten off more than we could chew! Our cows were milking well and at that time, milk was selling to the Milk Marketing Board, for four shillings a gallon.

Strangely enough, petrol was also at four shillings a gallon... We calculated that after all costs including repayments had been removed, that left us with one shilling a gallon (4.5 litres) clear. This was sustainable and we had great hopes of paying off some of the capital that our friend had invested.

It is strange in life, how just as you think things are fine, life decides to show you that you have no control and pushes your head under the water. This has happened on several occasions, so much so that I began to think that it was best not to give life the satisfaction of laughing at you and just assume things will probably get worse.

We were reasonably happy and content in our own little way, working like lunatics, with very little to show for it, when a bombshell was dropped. The estate agent "friend" decided that he was going to expand his business and he also wanted to purchase a life bond to cover his retirement. He was going to realise the cash by selling our two farms. This was total disaster, but to heap on more trauma, the Milk Marketing Board decided that there was too much milk being produced and lowered the price by one shilling a gallon, a drop of twenty five per cent. This was our shilling, without this we could not continue.

This was a time in my life when I, Dad, Mum, and Chris to a lesser extent, because he was getting married, all became very depressed. We had worked for nine years and now had nothing to show for it. The farm and all the stock were sold, along with all the equipment and workshop tools. As the milk price was so low, farm prices were also depressed, along with stock and equipment. We were just able to clear our commitments, but there was very little left.

Mum's mother and father had moved to Devon several years earlier and as her mother had died, we moved in with Granddad. This was a good arrangement, as he was getting a bit shaky, and had a heart problem. We had a small amount of money left after the farm sale, and Chris thought that we could do some contract work, ditching and removing banks and levelling sites. I was sceptical, as we had already tried contracting before and had found it tedious persuading farmers to part with their money. However, he persuaded us that it would be fine, so we purchased a Caterpillar bulldozer, and a Ruston Bucyrus 10 ton drag line for ditching. Chris decided that he would drive the bulldozer, so I had to use the back actor ditcher. I had never used one of these machines before and I can assure you that there is a definite knack to using one. It's a lovely machine, it throbs gently away behind you and no matter what you do, it seldom has to sound as if it is making any effort at all. My first job was to dig a very large hole for a septic tank. Great! I thought, I will have plenty of room to manoeuvre and digging a square hole should be a doddle! It wasn't quite that easy. I lowered the bucket gently to the ground and engaged the winch to wind in the cable. 10 R.B's are all worked by cables, miles of it! It really was quite impressive, a large strip of turf and soil disappeared inside the bucket, this is easier than I expected. With a back actor, to empty the bucket, the arm has to be extended, so the bucket is inverted. Easy? Well, not really, as the arm extended, the bucket hit the ground, at this point the bucket stopped, but the cable beside me in the cab didn't. There was a tremendous rattling and churning and yards and yards of thick cable started to fill the cab. I can say now that I did jump out of the cab, just as the end of the cable was reached. One may think that when the end was reached, the cable would stop, but no such luck, it then starts to rewind the cable the wrong way round and as the cable is running loose, it winds it in a most haphazard way! When all had gone quiet I crept back into the cab, how on earth do I sort this lot? I thought. The cab was nearly full of wire cable about three centimetres thick, or as it was then, about one inch thick. It took many hours to sort the tangle out; the cable was made of high tensile steel and went where it wanted to go, not where I put it. This was a very fast lesson in what not to do and as I learn quite fast, especially when I had to sort that lot out, I never had this problem again. Certainly not on such a grand scale.

We worked for about a year at this, during this time Chris was married and moved into a static caravan which we had to purchase from our meagre income. Times were still difficult and we were still having great difficulty getting in the money for the work we had done. The worry was affecting Dad quite a lot, I think that he felt that he had failed, but one thing we had gained was a vast amount of experience. Some of this experience was in how not to do things, but this can be just as valuable! Dad developed stomach ulcers along with lung cancer; he had always been a heavy smoker. I was, by this time, more than a little peeved. Chris was living with his wife and so had to have cash for living and other expenses. This left me with nothing.

So I made a decision, I was going to work for someone else, take my wages and let them worry; I'd had enough of this. I was twenty seven, no money, no job, not had a girl friend since I was thirteen and I was revolting. At this time Chris also decided to get a job, and went to work for a farm a few miles away, with a house that went with the job, so he was now fine and kept that job until he retired at sixty five.

We now lived in the village, so it was only a short walk to get anything we needed. I applied for a job, but to get to interviews, I would need some form of transport. I had fifteen pounds saved from my Christmas present that Grandpa had given me, so I bought a Ford Anglia for twelve pounds. It was a bit rough, but it started well, as long as their wasn't any sea mist about. It didn't like sea mist and as we did get a goodly share of these, I did spend some time cursing the thing.

It was on a grey day in February, a week before my twenty seventh birthday, that it happened. It was one of those events that stay with you for the rest of your life. I'd had a very painful stomach ache all day and by evening I couldn't stand properly. It was when I started vomiting that it was deemed necessary to call the doctor. After poking and prodding, the diagnosis was appendicitis. It was agreed that Dad would take me straight into Bideford hospital, about fourteen miles away. We arrived there at about eight o'clock and I was booked in and allocated a bed. It seems unbelievable, but this was the first time in all my life that I had slept away from my parents. I was slightly apprehensive, but also felt strangely liberated. I didn't have to answer to anyone, or justify my actions to anyone, I felt a strange relief.

As I lay in bed the following morning, waiting for the surgeon to visit, there was a change of staff and the Staff Nurse who took over the ward looked quite interesting. Now I hadn't had any girl friend, or indeed, any female relationships in my life, so it is possible that anything female would have looked interesting, but somehow this one appealed more so than any of the others. I had no idea what to do about it, but as this was an all male ward, I decided to involve some of the other patients, in how to approach someone you liked. Needless to say, there was plenty of advice given, some of which was certainly not appropriate. The chap in the next bed knew her and assured me she was single and lodged with a friend of his. Well, that's a start. Luckily for me, as I was not very speedy at approaching females, the stay in hospital after an appendectomy was two weeks, so I did have a day or two to hone these skills. I pondered long hours trying to work out what to do and how she would react to approaches from an out of work farmer. By this time, all sixteen men in the ward knew of my feelings and I was receiving advice from all directions. Some of this advice was too crude to put in print, but I think they meant well.

It was the day before my discharge from hospital that the opportunity arose. The Staff Nurse, whose name I discovered was Yvonne, was to remove my stitches. It was now or never. I had butterflies in my stomach and my mouth was dry, but in a quivering voice I asked "Would you like to go to the pictures on Saturday?" To my relief and the relief of five men huddled the other side of the curtain she said "Yes." I was relieved, elated and many more adjectives, but also a little bit anxious, she knew nothing about me, that I was a penniless out of work bloke who now had three months of inability to do heavy work. What had I done?

It was a very wet and cold evening, two days after my Birthday, when I drove my Ford Popular to Bideford for our rendezvous. We arrived at the cinema together, I had difficulty recognising her, as I had only seen her in uniform before and she was wearing a plastic rain hood to protect her newly permed hair. We each paid for ourselves, for which I was truly grateful, as my only finances in the world was a ten pound note that Grandpa had given me for my Birthday. We saw a Norman Wisdom film, I can't remember which, but we both laughed at the same places, so things were going well. After the pictures, she invited me to her digs for coffee. This was all new ground to me. I had to learn fast. I did!

I had told Mum and Dad of where I was going and who I was going to meet, so, on arrival home, questions were asked. I just replied that we had a lovely evening and good night. I suppose they were quite anxious for me, they knew that I was very green when it came to females. On leaving her digs we had agreed to meet the following weekend, so all was going well for the time being.

We met for several weeks and our favourite spot to go was Castle Hill in Torrington. We both loved it there, with views across the hills for miles, and a river running along the valley at the bottom. Indeed it was on the side of Castle Hill, one balmy April evening, six weeks after our first meeting, that I asked Yvonne to marry me. To my great relief she gave a positive reply and I was on cloud nine! Of course, on returning home I had to tell Mum and Dad, and they were very pleased, we celebrated with the only alcohol that was in the house, sherry, but why not? It had been a very good day all round and I was a very happy bunny. But, I still had to get work. I would put my mind to this tomorrow, and savour the happiness of today. In my life there hadn't been many occasions when I had felt so pleased with myself, and my life.

The work I knew best was of course, farming, but I did consider anything; I would have a wife to support. A farmer about nine miles away, was advertising for a tractor driver. As I was equipped with the necessary skills, I applied and was accepted on the spot. The wage was ten pounds a week, plus overtime. Not a great wage, but it was a start. I was now, for the first time in my life, in charge of my own destiny, as far as anyone ever is. This was the first time that I had money of my own to spend as I wanted. What bliss! After I had been at the farm for two weeks, I was given an extra two pounds a week and allowed to put four gallons of petrol in my car and charge it to his account. Things were looking good! The owners' son, who ran the day to day workings of the farm, was due to have a hernia operation. This gave me an opportunity to have vast amounts of overtime. They were long days, but I was used to that, and for the first time I had some savings. During these times when there was extra work, I saw little of Yvonne, just snatched periods when I returned home. Yvonne decided that she would like to move in with us so that we would at least see one another in the morning before work and again in the evening, although it was usually gone ten o'clock when I returned. She now had a fourteen mile ride to Bideford on her Honda 50. We discussed marriage plans and Yvonne thought that she would like a spring wedding. I am afraid I was a little less patient and suggested December. There was a house for rent on one of the local farms so we had more or less decided to live there. Yvonne was persuaded and a December wedding was agreed. By that time, the hernia patient would be fit again, and all the summer harvest would be over. It was an exciting time for me and Yvonne, and we really became very good friends.

Of course there were the usual traumas on the farm, not the least with the owner's son, Richard. He wasn't an easy person to work with, very self opinionated and apt to get very angry for little or no reason. As the herdsman had Tuesdays off, Richard had to milk the cows on that day. Richard hated milking and the cows were fully aware of it. It's the same with all animals, if they smell fear; they will react, usually aggressively. These cows were no exception and Tuesday's became a dreaded day of the week. Problems usually started on Monday evening, the more Richard thought about the following day, the more morose and horrible he became. Tuesday mornings I arrived at the farm with apprehension, not knowing what to expect. I knew that the day wouldn't be a good one when I saw the Land Rover parked in the middle of the lawn, not the usual parking spot. As I rounded the corner into the yard, I noticed pieces of the concrete blocks from the milking parlour were scattered everywhere. What on earth had happened? There was no sign of Richard, milking was finished or had ceased for some reason, what was going on? I went to the farmhouse door to enquire as to the whereabouts of Richard and as to whether milking was in fact finished or was there some temporary hold up. A very tearful wife appeared at the door and this is the story she told me:

Richard was awoken at five by his alarm clock; he was in a very bad mood as he hadn't slept much because he had been worrying about the milking. He appeared to blame the alarm clock for this and threw it through the closed window, with the effect that one would expect. He dressed and went to bring in the cows who had decided to move to new pastures during the night. After getting them in and by this time being late, he started to milk, but the electricity went off, so he had to put the tractor on the generator, all this time he was getting angrier and angrier, he started to shout and holler at the cows, they moved hastily to the other end of the yard where a weak gate gave way, and the milked and not milked cows were reunited. Now this is every cowman's nightmare. The only thing to do is put them all back through the parlour once more. Richard was doing this when the tractor running the generator ran out of fuel. It seems that this was the last straw, his senses left him. He let all the cows out in the field, milked and not milked together, switched all the equipment off, got into the Land Rover and drove to goodness knows where at stupid speeds, came back with a large sledge hammer and proceeded to try and knock the milking parlour down. He had returned at such a speed that he was unable to stop until the Land Rover wheels sank into the soft lawn. His reply to her when she innocently asked if anything was wrong was the reason for the tears and I cannot put his reply down on paper. He had now gone to bed with a migraine. Oh goody, this meant that I would have to sort out the mess, as his migraines usually lasted for three days or so. It wasn't a good day for me then, the parlour and milking machine had not been cleaned, half the cows had not been milked, so they would be very full and uncomfortable at night. The tractor needed the fuel problem sorting out, the yard gates had to be repaired and I was on my own. Richard's wife took pity on me and worked hard to sort things out. Now **I** was beginning to hate Tuesday's with a passion!

There were many Tuesdays of a similar ilk, but the rest of the week, things usually went well, we got on well together. We worked hard and long hours, but at least I was earning a reasonable wage. Of course, as soon as a small amount was saved, something would crop up to help you get rid of it. My ancient Ford finally expired, so I purchased an elderly Morris 8 series E. This was quite old, but there were no M.O.T's to worry about then. It was running well, and would get me to work and back each day, a round trip of eighteen miles. Our nearest town was

Bideford, and we went there at weekends for some of our requirements. There was a small problem with the car which I soon found out. Under the bonnet was a holder screwed to the inside wing of the car, containing a two pint bottle of oil. Every four gallons of petrol required one pint of oil to be poured into the engine. I thought that this was a bit too much and oil was quite expensive, so I decided to replace the piston rings. These old vehicles were much easier to deal with than modern cars, so this wouldn't be too difficult.

I started the following Sunday morning; I had only the one day to complete the task as I would need transport to work on Monday. To carry out the task properly, I decided to take out the engine, only a few bolts. These bolts were soon removed and the engine was ready to remove. It wasn't easy, but I was very strong then and I managed to raise the engine over the wing and lower it onto waiting blocks. As the day progresses I managed to replace the piston rings and at seven o'clock at night the engine was ready to be replaced. I heaved said engine over the vehicle wing and lowered it into place. Now came the tricky bit. To remove bolts is relatively easy, you unscrew them and they fall out, but to replace them is a different matter altogether. No matter how I tried I could not line up the holes. I struggled for a very long time, but no matter how I tried, the holes just needed to be moved one way or another. Finally, in desperation, I tied a rope under the engine and passed it over my shoulders and tied it. I was now able to raise or lower the engine in small amounts by lifting my back slightly. After several attempts, one of the bolts caught in the threads, and screwed in. I was extremely relieved but my back has not been the same since. Another one of my "do not try this at home," anecdotes. It was nearly midnight when I had finished, but the car started fine and ran nicely, so I was quite satisfied with my days work. The next morning when I awoke, my back did protest long and severely, but I thought it would get better when I started work. It did, but I am still having a lot of discomfort with it to this day, a reminder of my engine replacement days.

As the time moved on into November, we both became excited about our forthcoming marriage on December 3rd 1966, but that is another chapter!

Our wedding day

Chapter Seven

Yvonne and I get Wed.

Richard, as I have mentioned before, wasn't the easiest person in the world to get on with. He seemed to have a form of jealousy that meant that he would try and spoil any occasion that we had planned. Our wedding was to be on Saturday and then I was to have a week's holiday for our honeymoon. I wanted the Friday before the wedding off as well, but he said that if I wanted the week after my wedding, then I must work the Friday. So I agreed, I wouldn't have done so in today's world. I intended to leave early, but Richard had other ideas making sure that I had to work on quite late. Yvonne was not best pleased when I arrived back at seven o'clock.

Our wedding day dawned cold and grey, not a good omen. The ceremony was for midday and then a very small reception at the Bradworthy inn. Money was very scarce, we hadn't had time to save, and there were expenses to be met. We had seventy pounds to spend, this had to pay for our honeymoon, petrol, buy Christmas presents for both families and leave sufficient funds for our living expenses on our return. There were no Visa cards or Barclay cards at that time; you had to live within your means. Bank overdrafts were only obtained by an interview with the bank manager and having a guarantor for the loan. This was so that if we were unable to pay the loan back, they had someone else who would do so. We didn't intend to get into debt, so always paid as we went along.

The wedding was a simple church affair, with just family and a few friends. The reception was small, sixteen of us all together I think, we had a simple buffet, sandwiches, sausage rolls and of course a cake. Yvonne had borrowed her wedding dress from a nursing friend, and the cake was sold to her at cost price because she had nursed the baker. All this helped immensely to reduce costs. As we left the reception at about two thirty, the sky was dark and leaden and flurries of snow were stinging our faces. The car that we were going to use was a newly purchased Austin A40 Somerset; the Morris eight wasn't really suitable now as we were travelling to Yvonne's parents and sisters in Kent. This was about three hundred miles and no motorways!

We had nothing arranged for our honeymoon; we were just going to head towards the south coast of Cornwall. We set off with the usual tin cans rattling on behind, these were soon disposed of. We went about 50 miles or so, it was getting dark, and the snow was beginning to drift across the road making driving difficult. Bodmin was the next town; we decided that we would go to the best hotel in the town for our wedding night. The car was parked and it was not too difficult to see which the best hotel was, the Royal Hotel was the only one open. We booked in and were told the cost would be £5.00 a night. Ouch, at this rate, our finances would be very difficult to manage. This we decided would do for the one night, but was too much money for us to stay longer.

The room was very basic, no en-suite bathrooms then! The fan heater required half crowns (twelve and a half p.) to be fed into it every half an hour; the bathroom was at the far end of a long corridor. We settled down, pulling eiderdown tight round us and eventually fell asleep. At about two p.m. Yvonne decided that a visit to the facilities was essential. I pulled the covers over and dozed off again, but only for a very short while. I heard a loud bump, followed by some rather strong oaths. I pricked up my ears, but decided that it was very cold and I would find out eventually what had happened. A little while later Yvonne returned muttering gently. Evidently, because we were the only customers, the passage lights had been turned off, no doubt to save money. Half way along the corridor was a deep step, which Yvonne had forgotten. She had fallen down said step and was not a happy bunny.

Sunday morning dawned bright and clear, we had breakfast, paid the bill, and went looking for cheaper and hopefully better accommodation. We went south and ended up in West Looe, a very pretty little town. There were several bed and breakfast places, so we choose one and knocked on the door of a quaint fisherman's cottage. We were welcomed in and shown to a lovely warm room with comfortable bed and a stone hot water bottle in the bed, sheer luxury! The B&B was run by two elderly ladies called Mac and Ida. Which was which I never knew? The breakfasts were superb and the cost would be 18/6d (about £1.00) a night and if we stayed for the week there would be a rebate. This was more like it; our finances were going to be sufficient after all. We spent happy days at East and West Looe, the two were separated by the river, and a small ferry transferred us across. The weather stayed cold but bright, a delight. One day we drove to Plymouth, to purchase our Christmas presents. We had lunch in Woolworths and I had the best cream doughnut that I have ever had. I always said that it was the highlight of the honeymoon for me. This comment does cause a little irritation with said wife. One problem with staying in a quiet village in December is what to do in the evenings.

Luckily there was a local pub, very quiet, just a couple of fishermen, but they played all the latest records. These have become our most favourite and memorable tunes. Tom Jones with The Green, Green, Grass and Tie a Yellow Ribbon, also The Beach Boys with Good Vibrations and several more that were popular at that time. We remember our simple and cheap honeymoon, with great pleasure and fondness; life seemed to be a little simpler then, and more of a gentle pace. I suppose every generation has similar feelings.

We returned to Bradworthy on the twelfth of December, laden with presents and very happy. A cottage on a local farm had been rented for the winter, as it was usually let to summer holiday makers. The cottage was quaint, but very damp, really wet more than damp. We could lie in bed and watch the water running down the inside walls. We purchased an electric blanket, just to keep the bed dry. While we had been on honeymoon, Yvonne's sister, her husband and three children had stayed in the cottage. They had left a note saying that they had blocked up all the holes where the wind was blowing in. They had also left confetti in most unusual and irritating places. On flushing the toilet, a shower of confetti rained down. All the cupboards were also similarly primed to catch out the unsuspecting. Oh well, such is families.

We had entered our name on the local council's waiting list for a council house. As luck would have it, new houses were being built at that time. During our wet and cold winter we had notification that we had been allocated one of these new dwellings. How lucky was that?

We moved into our lovely new home in May 1967. What a treat! It was lovely and warm and dry, nicely decorated, with a Rayburn cooker and hot water. Now we could start a family. The estate was also within easy walking distance of the village of Bradworthy, so Yvonne could get all our needs there. Also Mum and Dad were only a stones throw away, so were able to baby sit or help if needed.

I still worked at Morwenstow, about nine miles away, but I didn't mind the travelling. As I was a tractor driver, I didn't have to get to work until eight o'clock. As the summer progressed and the work load increased, I was arriving home after ten o'clock at night, making very long days. The overtime pay was very useful and Richard's father had given me another rise to cover our council house rent. This was two pounds a week.

Things progressed reasonably well at Cornakey Farm, Richard and I had our differences, but I am afraid I usually gave in to him as it made life much easier. On October 31st 1968 our first son Anthony Thomas was born. He was born in Barnstaple Hospital, over 30 miles away from where we lived. I was so spaced out about having a son, that it wasn't until I had driven the 30 miles home on a wet and very dark night, that I realised that I hadn't dipped the headlights all the way home, I did wonder why so many cars flashed their lights at me. We had a great winter and summer following Tony's birth. We had to get used to being a family. I did start to become a little upset, I wasn't seeing very much of Tony. He was mostly still asleep when I left and had gone to bed when I returned. I mostly worked on Saturdays as well, so all in all it was far from ideal.

The following summer was an even more labour intensive one than ever, Richard had more and more migraines and the weather was very unpredictable. On many occasions, I didn't see Tony from one weekend to the next. This wasn't what we wanted for a family life. At this time the cowman at Cornakey left, and Yvonne and I discussed whether it would be good for me to take on the herdsman's job. There was a house that went with the position, so there would be no extra cost there. I wouldn't have an hour a day travelling. I would start at six o'clock, but be back for breakfast at nine. Back in again at midday and finish at six. The main point against it was that although I was capable of doing the work, I didn't like milking cows. After much deliberation we decided that the move would improve our family life, and the pay was better. These were two very important points that outweighed the others. We lived in Bradworthy for two years before we moved to Yeolmouth, the name of the tied cottage that we then moved into. This was an isolated property, about two miles off the Morwenstow road. We were a lot nearer the sea than the road. Cornakey Farm land bordered the Atlantic Ocean, with towering cliffs over three hundred feet high. As a tractor driver, I loved to take my lunch out to the cliff tops and just watch the sea. It was never the same, varying from peaceful, lapping waves to gigantic, streaming rollers that sent foam and froth up to the very top of these majestic cliffs. The winter gales were a thing to behold. When checking animals that were in the cliff fields, on very windy days they would all be laying along the cliff edge. The force of the wind rushing up the cliff face meant that near the edge there was actually a slight amount of wind blowing towards the sea. This caught me out the first time that I checked stock in these conditions. As I approached the cliff edge, I was nearly in a horizontal position, leaning hard into a gale force ten. On reaching the cattle, I found that I was being pulled towards the edge of the cliff. I was extremely lucky; I stopped because I fell over a recumbent heifer. As I lay on the ground, I pondered on what had nearly occurred, I can say now that I was very pleased that the heifer had been lying in just the right position. One of my lucky occasions!

Bradworthy Church

Me trying to thatch a rick

Back to elavator to unload at the clamp

Making silage, circa 1956. Green crop loader and muscle power

Chapter Eight

Milking Cows and Yeolmouth

We moved to Yeolmouth on a crisp and frosty morning in March. We used a tractor and trailer to carry our not too plentiful amount of furniture. Nearly all of our furniture was purchased by Dad, at Bradworthy furniture auction. Yvonne and I had asked him to buy items for us. He had to stop work because of ill health, so it gave him something to do and something else to think about. We had bought a new bed and a new mirror. Mostly every thing else was second hand and very cheap. Yeolmouth was a solidly built stone and slate house that had once been two very small houses. The rooms had a strange layout, as it was necessary to go through two of the rooms to reach the others. No problem when family is staying, but as the toilet was on the ground floor it wasn't so nice passing through bedrooms with sleeping bodies in. As I have said, Yeolmouth was near the cliffs, and therefore was the first immovable object the Atlantic gales struck. Even though the house was stone built, in severe gales it was possible to feel the house shake when struck by a particularly heavy gust of wind. We did, on more than one occasion, come downstairs to find all the doors wide open. This was caused by the frequent shaking and movement of the house. The first time we couldn't really believe it, but Richard said that it often happened in gales. Unless these conditions have been experienced, it seems unbelievable. On one occasion, Yvonne was just putting a shovel of coal on the open fire when I opened the back door. The force of the wind caused such an up draught in the chimney that the coal went up the chimney and was never seen again! Our coal stock of maybe several hundred weights would be transferred twenty yards or more overnight. We had some good times at Yeolmouth as well. Tony was growing up quite fast, and now Yvonne was expecting our second child.

Yvonne's family lived in Herne Bay, Kent. We would travel to them for holidays and breaks; they would come to us on some occasions. The distance was about three hundred miles, and there were no motorways. The roads we had to travel on through Barnstaple, Bampton and Wiveliscombe to Taunton were notoriously bad. The journey usually took about ten hours. The best time to travel was after work and in the dark. I would come in from milking at six o'clock; Yvonne would have the car loaded and ready to go. A quick tea and wash and change and we left about seven. A small child would be asleep in the back of the estate car, where we had put a mattress. Cot on the roof rack and off we would go. We would arrive at Yvonne's sisters at six in the morning. I certainly wouldn't appreciate such a journey now. The most tiring of these trips, was going to Herne Bay for Yvonne's father's funeral. I could only get cover for my milking job for two days. We left as before, Yvonne went to the funeral; I stayed at her sisters with Tony. We left again at six o'clock at night, got back to Yeolmouth at nine o'clock in the morning. The journey had been atrocious, fog all the way across Salisbury Plain. I will not forget that trip and I had to milk the cows that same night!

I have mentioned that Cornakey was situated on the cliff edge. This brought with it some marvellous benefits and some severe drawbacks. It was possible to reach the sea by an extremely steep and winding cliff path. It was really only suitable for goats. It really was very dangerous, with a narrow ledge clinging to the cliffs and a sheer drop of hundreds of feet on the other. In some places the path had disappeared into the foaming brine below. Richard had gone down to the beach on several occasions and had bought back various items of flotsam and jetsam. He convinced me that we could easily get down to the beach, have a dip and return in our lunch hour. I believed him. I had good balance and plenty of strength then and it was, to put it mildly, a precarious and downright dangerous journey.

As we approached the small cove, which was completely inaccessible from any other direction, we could see that the whole of the pebble beach above high tide was six to eight feet deep in timber, all sawn ten feet long and mostly four inches by four inches. This is a most useful size, and can be used for many jobs on a farm. It so happened that we had just started building work on a new milking parlour and this was exactly the size required to construct the loft and roof, and all for nothing. Richard got very excited and started collecting some of the pieces of wood together and tied them with some blue nylon rope that was also lying about. I was puzzled, it had been bad enough coming down empty handed, but to climb back up with ten feet lengths of sea soaked timber was ludicrous. Richard pointed out that it was a lot easier going back up than coming down. I was sceptical, but if he wanted to carry them up and literally risk his life, there would be no way that I could talk him out of it. He tied about ten pieces together and tried to carry them, but the load was well over a hundredweight and quite impossible to carry up the narrow path. He split the bundle into two and said would I take half. Common sense told me "no", but I was a lot younger and I did like a challenge. We started up the winding path with our precarious loads, staggering and swearing every time the wood got stuck in the cliff face or under rocks. It was a slow tiring and dangerous trek and just under halfway up we came to where the path had fallen away. It was impossible to transverse this ten feet stretch with our load. We decided to leave our bundles and cross this stretch and then drag the timber across afterwards with our blue nylon rope. We scrambled across and started to haul our cargo across. As the wood left the security of its rocky ledge, it started to roll down the cliff. We had to release the rope and watch our precious timber go crashing back down to the beach from whence it came. Now we must learn from our mistakes, so, for our second load, it was agreed that I would go back and stop the load from rolling seawards. I retraced my steps and grabbed the wood; I had decided that I would stay on the uphill side, so that I would just let it go if I thought it was too dangerous. With much heaving and straining we managed to inch our load across the steep precipice and to the relative security of the narrow path. We did eventually arrive at the top and collapsed with exhaustion. The whole exercise had been fraught with danger and I, for one, would not undertake this beach combing again. At this time, the cowman that was leaving Cornakey was still living on the farm, prior to taking on a council smallholding. He was an ingenious fellow and was always on the lookout for ways of making money. Richard said that he would pay him £1 for each length of wood that he recovered from the beach. The cowman jumped at this opportunity for some easy cash! He only did the trip once; he decided that life was too good to risk in such a way. We found later that night that a timber carrying ship had lost its load just off the Cornish coast. Hence the reason for our wood covered beach.

I did go down to the Cornakey beach on one other occasion. I had been sitting on the cliff edge enjoying my lunch and the magnificent views when I decided to look down onto the beach. To do this it was necessary to go right to the cliff edge, lay on a large flat rock and just put ones head over the precipice. I was puzzled to see what looked like a heap of clothes on the pebbles. It was a beautiful clear day and the beach was in a spotlight of bright sunlight. As I looked, I imagined that the clothes were, in fact a person, laying there. The position of the person suggested that, if it was a person, they most certainly weren't sun bathing. There were no mobile phones then, I was a long distance from the farmhouse and I knew that Richard and Margaret weren't at home. This was the reason for me taking a longer than usual lunch break! The only thing I could really do was to investigate. I set off along the reasonably easy start to the walk, but when I arrived at the most difficult area, I could see a lot of recently loosened stones. The moss was loose and lifted off of the cliff sides. From this point, and indeed from any point while descending the track, it wasn't possible to see the beach. This didn't become visible until the last few yards. I continued down as fast as possible, which really was quite slowly, I didn't wish to end up a casualty of these cliffs. On reaching the beach, a very sorry sight was before me. A woman of, I suppose thirty or so was indeed the pile of clothes I had seen. She had obviously fallen from the track where I had seen the loose rocks. She was obviously well past any assistance and I now wondered what my next move should be. It was at this time, right on cue that the R.A.F. helicopter from Coldrose appeared round the corner of the bay. It hovered over head and a medic was lowered. He was slightly puzzled as to what I was doing there, as their records showed Cornakey Bay as being inaccessible from the cliffs. I quickly explained and he inspected the woman. A stretcher was lowered and the body taken up to the top of the cliffs and laid on the grass in our field. I then had to climb back up the path, feeling much shaken. Now I could really see how a mistake on these cliffs would end.

I successfully negotiated the path back and on appearing over the top, saw that an ambulance, the coastguard a mountain rescue team and the police, were in attendance. The body was still lying where it had been placed and covered with a blanket. I was very interested to know how and why the rescue helicopter had been summoned, although extremely relieved that it had, its appearance at the right time had solved my problem as what my next move would have been. The policeman explained that a man and a woman had set off from Welcome Bay, about two miles north of Cornakey, and were following the Cornish coastal footpath. At the top of the cliffs at Cornakey, they couldn't find the path, and had mistakenly taken our little cliff track. Halfway down, the woman had lost her footing and fallen to her death. The man, obviously, scared out of his wits, had come back up the cliff and hailed some other walkers who had guided him to the road and a telephone. By this time Richard had returned and wondered what all the activity was, as all the vehicles had to go through the farm yard. This experience was an extremely sobering one to me and I vowed that I would not go to Cornakey beach again.

I have mentioned that we were building a new milking parlour, this, Richard and I were undertaking during our "quieter periods". We were constructing everything ourselves, from excavation of the pit to building the interior walls, putting in the loft and all loft machinery. The only part that we were not attempting was the installation of the milking equipment. This was a major undertaking, but I had the skills that I had learnt at Blatchborough to see me through. Richards's father, who was an architect, followed our progress with wry comments. We made a good job and the parlour worked well when I milked in it. However, Richard was still relieving me on Tuesdays and he did not improve with his technique or temper. I dreaded coming into work on Wednesdays, there would be a list a foot long of problems that he had occurred, most of which he either said or hinted at, were my fault. However, no job is perfect and I had a good home life to escape to.

Richard went through a very unsettled period and his home life and work were deteriorating.

We worked hard, but I had some rewarding times. I had always been pretty good with mechanical equipment and there wasn't much that I enjoyed more that stripping down an engine and rebuilding it. I was able to use my mechanical skills, when the engine driving the water pump broke down. This was a critical piece of tackle, as all the water for the farm was drawn up from a bore hole one hundred and eighty feet deep. The engine used was a one and a half horse power petrol/paraffin engine that ran for about six hours every day. It had become difficult to start and made a lot of rumbling noises. I spent the whole of one day and half the night rebuilding it. I started at the top and worked down replacing all moving parts. It was a mammoth job to complete in one day, I wasn't at all sure that I could manage the task before the farm ran out of water. A hundred cows use a vast amount of water, drinking at least ten gallons per cow, plus water for washing parlour and household use. It was ten thirty when Richard and I replaced the engine on its base plate, connected the drive belt and started it up. It was a most rewarding moment also a moment of relief. The engine started immediately and ran as sweet as a nut, no rattles or rumbles. I was very tired, but had a feeling of satisfaction. I revisited the farm five years later; the engine was still running well.

There was great competition between Richard and myself. Richard always wanted to drive the biggest tractor; he said it was because he would do more work. On many occasions, I could go to places and across fields better with my smaller vehicle, which he was not best pleased about. We had many weight carrying competitions, to see who could carry the most sacks at a time and so on. I usually won these competitions and Richard ended up saying that I must be the strongest man in Cornwall. This came about mainly because he couldn't park his car neatly on the roadside. He could have a forty feet clear space, but when he got out, one end of the vehicle would be two feet away from the kerb. It was on one of these occasions that we alighted to see that the rear of the car was miles away from the kerb. Richard muttered that he supposed he had better try again, I said that there was no need to bother, picked up the rear end of his car and put it neatly against the kerb. He was somewhat surprised and I had to carry out this manoeuvre on several occasions. No wonder I suffer from a bad back now!

We had some very amusing occurrences. We didn't have a serviceable cattle crush, so a lot of the animal husbandry jobs were carried out rodeo style. We would take turns to select an animal and then pursue it round the yard until we caught it. This was not an easy task even with the smaller cattle, but when we were worming eighteen month old heifers, weighing six or seven hundredweight, the job became very interesting. It was our practice to always start with the smallest, and worked up, the theory being that we would get used to the heavier animals gradually. The trouble with this theory is that one also gets more tired and weaker. It was nearing the end of our rodeo session; the animals were quite large and heavy. I ran along beside one of the largest animals, got a grip on her short stubby horns and pulled her to the ground. The exertion had caused my false teeth to eject from my mouth and they were now beneath a very large heifer. Richard was having hysterics and was completely unable either to drench the animal or help me reacquire my dentures. It was some time before I could get any sense or help from him.

It was after I had worked with Richard for about five years that his father decided that he wanted to sell Cornakey and purchase a property in Suffolk. I was really quite settled at the time, but not too upset, jobs were reasonably easy to find at that time. Our second son, Timothy was born on the fifth of July 1971. A big lad!

I had been through the experience of a farm sale before. It was not an experience that I had enjoyed. All the animals have names or numbers, and a character that we all accept and become acclimatised to. Like people, we had learnt to accept their idiosyncrasies. Obviously some were more endearing than others, but we had learnt to accept them all and they were part of our lives. We now had to see them sold to the highest bidder. It is a sad experience. The day came and I was given the job of moving the cattle round the ring and giving her details, such as, when she had calved, if she was in calf, milk yield and any problems that they might have. It was a sad day, but it went well and everything that was for sale was sold, at a reasonably satisfactory price. Richard's family and his parents moved out one week later, as there was no milking, I had been given the task of cleaning up everything for the new owner.

The farm was sold to a local farmer, he had two sons and intended for his eldest son to run Cornakey.

He asked me to stay on, but he didn't intend to have milking cows so could not match my present earnings. Yvonne and I pondered for sometime and decided that we would stay for a while, during which time we would check to see what jobs were about. At this time, some well paid herdsmen jobs in New Zealand were being advertised in the Farmers Weekly. Here was a thought. Obviously there were drawbacks, leaving Mum and Dad was one. Dad insisted that if we wanted to go, then, go for it. I applied and was offered a good position as herd manager of five hundred cows, at a good salary. We applied for our immigration papers, which duly arrived. On reading, it appalled me to read, *"All immigrants must wrap belongings in a large woollen blanket. This bundle would be opened and fumigated on arrival."* I don't know why, but we decided that perhaps New Zealand wasn't for us. This was a point in our lives, when our future could have taken a totally different path and who knows what would have been the consequences. I worked for Cornakey's new owner for about three months. It was boring. There were no real challenges and no future, as it became obvious that when the owner's second son was old enough and experienced enough, I would be surplus to requirements! I applied for several jobs as herdsman, this being the only farm job to pay sufficient wages. Tractor drivers pay was pitiful. We travelled the country from Devon to

Northumberland for interviews. We didn't like most of them, farmers seemed to be under the impression that, because there was a house with the position, it was of no consequence as to the condition of said house. There were vague promises of the house being modernised later, or a better house being available later. This was certainly not a secure enough offer to convince us of their sincerity.

It was about our third or fourth week of inspecting the Farmers Weekly, applying and being interviewed, that I noticed a herdsman's position was available at a Co-operative farm in Down Ampney near Cirencester. The remuneration looked good, as the more milk that I was able to produce, the more money I would get. This would give me a challenge, something that I have always needed. As the Co-operative had five dairy farms in Down Ampney and a lot of houses, finding suitable housing wouldn't be a problem. I knew that I would have to work extremely hard to receive a really good wage, but I was never afraid of working. I applied and went for an interview. When we arrived, the farm manager said that I was too experienced for the position that they had advertised. My heart sank. Why had I not been informed before travelling two hundred miles? He could see that I was a little vexed and hastily pointed out that a new milking parlour was being built and as I had experience of milking in a parlour, would I take this position? After we had talked and inspected the farm where the new parlour was being built and viewed the property which was being offered, I accepted. There was a great deal that needed attention on Home Farm. Many of the cattle were lame and a lot looked in poor health. Milk yields were abysmal and the staff were uncaring. What an opportunity, improving in these conditions was easy. If the farm had been on top form, I would have been more hesitant, as I would be paid on the amount of milk that the herd produced over their present production level. Yvonne and I pondered on the pros and cons of moving to Down Ampney and decided that it would be a good move. There were several reasons for this, of course the higher wage was a good incentive and certainly a good motivator, but there was also the fact that the Co-operative also had a good pension fund, there was a good opportunity to increase our income by herd improvement, the house offered was extremely good and I liked my line manager. There was one main fault and that was the school. It was very poor. As Tony was only four, we calculated that we could stay at Down Ampney for two to three years without causing too much of a problem. With the Co-operative, there was opportunity for advancement.

Let's do it! So it was on a lovely May morning we were moved to Down Ampney.

My long suffering, Mum. 1960

Dad 1939

Chapter Nine

Down Ampney, Cirencester, Glos.

Our move to Cirencester wasn't without its trauma. The manager from the Down Ampney estate had arranged our moving details, a cattle box was being sent from Gloucester to Cornwall to load our furniture and would be with us late morning. We would load our furniture that afternoon and evening and then leave Cornwall early the following morning. There would be no problem as the truck was brand new, this would be it's first long distance outing. We waited and waited on the appointed day and after many telephone calls, it arrived at six o'clock in the evening. It most certainly was not a brand new vehicle that pulled into the yard. It arrived in a cloud of steam and evil smelling fumes. The driver alighted and introduced himself as Billy Smart. I think smart by name and not by nature certainly applied in this case. Evidently, the new vehicle wasn't registered, as the tax disc hadn't arrived, so Billy had set off, not without some misgivings, on the two hundred mile journey. He had told the farm manager that there could be major problems, but as all was arranged for us to move, he considered that the risk was worth taking. I think that he was under the impression that the driver was exaggerating the problems. This was probably true. We heard stories from him of how he had to stop at every service station to cool off the engine. When I got to know him better over the next few months, I realised that he would stop for a cup of tea whenever he saw an opportunity. My theory later was that he drank several cups of tea at the first services, and then had to have a toilet stop at the next one; while he was there he had several cups of tea again and so progressed very slowly over the two hundred miles.

As he was so late arriving in Cornwall, it would be difficult to load all the furniture before nightfall. We worked hard and by ten thirty all was aboard apart from our bed, a bed for Billy and enough food for breakfast. We slept fitfully that night and when dawn came were not particularly refreshed. It would be a long day. We ate breakfast, loaded the last of our chattels and waved goodbye to Billy. We carried out the final cleaning and checking and set off in our Vauxhall Victor Estate car. Myself, Yvonne, Tony, Tim and George our wayward dog, along with a complete range of cleaning equipment, some food that had been left in cupboards, and an array of hardware that we had collected together, and then we said goodbye to Yeolmouth. We had some good times there. We were also now moving two hundred miles from Mum and Dad, but as Dad was driving, that was not too much of a problem. The house we were going to move into was large enough for them to stay with us.

We set off about nine thirty, Billy had left at seven, so would be well on his way. The first part of the journey is tedious, being made up of country roads and the A39 which went through Barnstaple, Bampton, and Wiveliscombe to Taunton. From Taunton to Cirencester was mostly motorway, the M5 was just completed, and at that time was not too crowded. We arrived in Down Ampney at about two o'clock not having seen our furniture anywhere along the way. He must have been in the services again. There were no mobile phones, so contact was impossible. When we arrived at the house we had been shown, we were met by the farm manager. There was a problem, the house that we had been offered was now being lived in by the ex farm manager. There was another house that would be available shortly; would we like to see it? We had little option, and we were not impressed by being shoved about like this. He took us to a lovely house that we both fell in love with immediately. There was a problem however; it was not available until the cowman that I was replacing retired, but until then, we would have to live in a two up and two down semi on the main road. What had I done? It did not give me much confidence in the management. Our boats were burnt, we could not go back, we would have to make the best of it, and ensure that the promises were kept. It was now five o'clock, and still no furniture. Ten hours was a very long time even for Billy! At eight thirty he rolled up with tales of boiling engines and other various details that we were too tired and irritable to ponder at that time. The farm manager had arranged for some of the farm staff, of which there were plenty, to assist with the unloading. They set about the job with a will, and soon all our furniture was piled on the lawn. It seemed that they had only been asked to help unload, and that is what they did. When the vehicle was empty, they disappeared like snow in the summer sun. We had collected more furniture while we were in Yeolmouth; the house was a good size. It was a bit like putting a quart in a pint pot. Yvonne and I had to carry all the stuff in on our own. The rooms were full, and there was still a large amount covering the lawn. As it was now quite late, we decided to sort out the boy's room, and put them to bed. This would allow us to bring in the rest of the stuff and pile it up in the centre of the living room. Remember, Tony was three and a half, Tim was nine months, and it had been a very long day. It was at this point that our new neighbour came in with sandwiches and tea, very welcome. It was nearly midnight when we had finished bringing everything into the house. Luckily it had been a dry day throughout, so nothing was wet or damaged. We dragged our weary limbs to bed and fell instantly asleep.

It was a beautiful sunny morning when we awoke; we all had slept well and felt much better for it. I had two days to sort everything out before I was expected to start at Home Farm. It was hectic, and there was no time to waste. Curtains to hang, cooker to connect, carpet to lay, the list was endless, and there was no way all the jobs could be completed in two days. We set a list of priorities and worked down it. At least after two days we were more or less ship-shape.

Home Farm, Down Ampney.

Home Farm was situated on a quiet cul-de-sac that was the approach road to the beautiful little Down Ampney church. The large flat fields surrounded the farm buildings and as the area had, at one time, been a part of the estate, groups of lime and poplars were dotted across the landscape. The large and magnificently maintained Down Ampney House was adjacent to the farm and as the cows had to pass the pristine lawns that were between the huge Cotswold stone walls and their track, I did receive a few complaints when cow footprints appeared on the velvet green lawns. During the 1939-1945 war, a large part of the farm had been converted to an air field and camp for R.A.F personnel. A great deal of the runway and taxi area was still under concrete.

This area was extremely useful for silage clamps and for building on as the concrete was very thick and no footings were necessary. The outside circular track was also quite good as a racetrack, I shall say no more! This was a beautiful area to live and work and it seemed that the sun shone most of the time, I'm sure that it didn't, but that is how I remember my time there.

At my interview, I had seen the farm, which looked extremely run down, but I hadn't met the staff. When I did meet them, it appeared that they were almost as run down as the farm. The cowman was a friendly enough chap, sixty five and about to retire. The tractor driver was of a similar ilk, the foreman was about sixty and obviously resented my being there. There were also two others who seemed to come and go when they felt like it. The cows were a sad bunch as well. The building that they were usually being milked in was now being converted into the new milking parlour, so the herd was being milked through a portable milking bail, (a portable, temporary parlour). To be honest, most of the cow's yields were so bad, they weren't really worth milking. I joined in as the cows were being milked, but there seemed to be so many bodies about that I was really superfluous. There were so many ooohs and aars, that I appeared to be in a foreign country. As the days progressed and I became used to the dialect, it was possible to understand most of what they were saying. Their ideas of obtaining the best results from cows were extremely outdated. They had no idea of feeding for yield, or indeed of feeding for anything. I struggled on working with them until the new parlour was finished. I certainly needed them to cajole the reticent cows into this new building. After a week or so I was able to milk on my own, there were only sixty cows at that time and now the new parlour was up and running I could get through milking in just over an hour. There was much ooohing and aaring about, but I was now running the farm on my own, just assistance with difficult calvings and muck spreading. I now had control of the feeding as well, so if things went wrong, it was my fault.

When the parlour was finished, the herdsman retired and moved out of his house to a smaller one in Latton. This meant that the house we liked and had been promised was vacant. I was not going to loose out this time, and immediately went to see the farm manager. He was hesitant at first, saying would it not be better to stay where we were. I pointed out that we had been promised that house and it was part of the contract. He did agree, so we soon moved into 48 Down Ampney. This was a beautiful detached

Cotswold stone house with super gardens. It was the best house we had ever had and things looked good.

As most of the cows had lost the best part of their yield during the change from shippon milking to bail milking to parlour milking, I thought it best to cut the losses, dry most off early and give them a good rest, ready to start their lactation in September and October when most were due to calve. This worked in two ways, firstly, their present lactation would be very bad, nothing to do with me, as I had only just taken over. Secondly, there was a good chance that after an extended rest or dry period, they would yield better the following year, when it was only up to me. The yields were abysmal for their lactations. Home Farm was the lowest of the six herds at Down Ampney, and also the lowest of all the Co-operative's thirty six herds in the country. Not a word was said to me, but I knew I would have to pull out all the stops for the next year or two.

I worked hard and long during those first months, we had a holiday booked for a week, but during the week I still went and checked the in-calf cows and fed them. By now I knew what the quality of the staff was and I wasn't going to take any chances. Our future depended on it. Yvonne was not happy about it, but she could see my reasoning and agreed. We just went out days after I had checked the girls in the morning and I looked at them again in the evening.

It was when these cows started to calve that it was obvious that my hard work had paid off. All were calving down looking really good and they were obviously going to milk well as long as we could obtain sufficient feed for them. During their previous lactation, the milk yields were only just over seven hundred gallons a cow, but now yields were considerably better and during the three years that I milked cows at Down Ampney, yields increased by three hundred and fifty gallons per cow. This sort of yield wasn't exceptional, but by this time, the Home Farm herd was top of the Down Ampney Estate herds and also the top yielding herd of all the Co-operative farms.

The elderly staff had now been moved to other jobs and I just had one rascal of a man helping me. He was what I would call a likeable rogue. He would never drop me into a difficult situation, his stock phrase was "I dunno you", which in translation meant that he had no idea of what was happening, where I was or what I was doing. This infuriated the various managers, of which there were three and they assumed that I hadn't told my assistant anything. This wasn't true, we both knew what each other was doing and it was just that he wouldn't divulge information in case it might incriminate either him self or me. The gentleman's name was Ron Cuss and he really could be an awkward cuss! He had been moved round the estate from farm to farm, but didn't fit in. I was his last chance of continuing on the estate and he appreciated this chance and worked well with me. He wasn't above creeping off behind the farm buildings for a smoke and it was on one of these occasions that he encountered a major difficulty. The first inclination I had of a problem was when I saw a scrawny, naked man run through the parlour. I was, to put it mildly puzzled and amused at this and thought that I had better follow him into the dairy. Ron was lying flat out completely naked in the dairy water trough. I wasn't particularly happy at this, as we have to be very strict on hygiene and bathing in the dairy water trough was definitely frowned upon. After a few seconds I noticed a selection of winged creatures circling the prostrate form, which was trying to sink every part of his body below the water level. It could be quite relevant to point out that Ron's stature was not large. He was a small scrawny little man of about five feet three inches, with skinny little legs and arms, his weight would not have been in excess of seven stone. The picture I had then of him still haunts the corners of my mind to this day. I think that at this point I should mention too, that Ron was not silent during this performance. A string of oaths were being uttered along with several ouches and howls. I opened the large dairy door and flapped around with the towel and eventually drove off the frenzied wasps that were attacking him. I handed the towel to Ron to dry him self, but I could not resist laughing. This didn't particularly amuse him, but he wasn't standing where I was and he did look a sorry sight. Bright red lumps were appearing over his legs and arms and it must have been very painful. He asked me to retrieve his clothes for him; they were strewn across the yard and round the back of the barn to a wasps nest. I was still puzzled as to what he had been doing there, it wasn't somewhere that there was any need to go. I took his clothes, after checking for any wasps still in residence, and enquired as to what had happened. Ron was very good with the apologetic, sheepish looks and this was one of the best I had seen. As it was a hot day and Ron wanted to smoke, he had decided to go behind the barn, light up and possibly have a snooze. He had been sitting there quite comfortably minding his own business, when he had become aware of a creeping swarm of wasps slowly moving up his legs. Of course, as we all would, he panicked. Ripping of his trousers, he jumped up and ran for the dairy water trough, strewing clothes as he went. Ron wasn't particularly surprised that I wasn't very sympathetic towards him, but I took pity on him and sent him home to get his wounds tended. I felt sure he had learnt a lesson, even if it was to make sure he didn't sit on a wasps nest again!

We did have several extremely amusing occurrences; they always seemed to happen to Ron. He would go onto the airfield to spread muck and return with just the drawbar attached to the tractor. I was stood at the dairy door at the time, I shouted to him to stop. When he did I asked him what had happened to the muck spreader. We were often teasing each other and he assumed I was doing this now. Without looking around, he grinned and said that it was behind the tractor, of course. I had to get quite cross before he decided to look behind him. He performed a hilarious double take. He knew that it was there and I was teasing him, so the first glance was quick and casual, still grinning. This glance was however enough for him to see that he was not indeed being followed by said muck spreader. The drawbar bolts had sheared off, and the wayward piece of equipment had travelled on a path of its own, ending up in a copse beside the concrete track. Ron had a keen sense of humour, sometimes a little on the wicked side, but when he started to play tricks on me, I was well up for the challenge. We kept a battery powered electric fencer in the shed beside the dairy. This shed housed the hot water boiler used for the parlour and dairy, also the milking machine switches. I had to enter it to turn off the milking machine. Ron was aware of this and had connected the electric fencer unit to the inside of the metal door handle. Now electric fencers are not dangerous, but they can wake you up with an involuntary oath or two. I could hear Ron cackling round the corner, so decided to say nothing. My time would come! Ron rode his bicycle to work, a metal frame on nice insulated rubber tyres. This was an opportunity I couldn't miss. I hid the fencer under some sacks and connected it to his bike. The response when he collected his bike at lunch time was well worth while and most rewarding. I'm afraid to say that the electric fencer was used by both of us on many occasions after that and not for the purpose for which it was intended.

Ron and his lovely daughter Patsy, who was thirteen, were very close and often had experiences that would have been frowned on if they were known about. It was just before Christmas and Ron wanted a Christmas tree. He decided that rather than buy one, he would fell one of the large fir trees and just use the top of it. There was a small wood on Home Farm in which there were some large fir trees. Just as it was getting dark they crept into the wood to select a suitable candidate. Tree selected, they set about felling it. They only needed the top, which was of a suitable dimension to fit in the front room. The base of the tree was quite thick and by the time the tree succumbed to their hard work it was quite dark. As the tree crashed to the ground, they were amazed to see electricity wires that were running through the wood, come crashing down as well. These wires supplied the electricity to half of Down Ampney, which was now enveloped in eerie darkness. Ron and Patsy picked up their tools and ran as fast as they could back to the safety of their dark home. It was a mystery that was never solved by the local inhabitants, I found out about it some time later when Ron had enjoyed a drink or two.

Most of the other workers at that time were rather introverted and distrusted strangers. We, as a family, were finding it difficult to become part of the community. I had taken the older cowmen's place; I was new and had new ideas. One doesn't trust strangers with new ideas; you don't know where it would end up. Eventually we were sort of accepted and as they realised that perhaps some of the new ideas were actually working, things began to improve. It was a very great time of change in agriculture, particularly for the Co-operative. New ideas in feeding, management, housing and general husbandry were being embraced at this time. The Co-operative estates were no exception and as they had become out dated and neglected, the changes were even more dramatic.

We were now living in a lovely Cotswold stone and slate detached house with beautiful gardens that surrounded it on three sides. It was number 48 Down Ampney, and had a double hedge between the garden and main road. Very old yew hedges made arches outside the back door and gave wonderful protection from wind and weather. We had a friendly Blackbird that hopped into the kitchen. Small Box hedges bordered the neat gravel paths, and the whole area had been landscaped well every morning. There was also a large vegetable garden, where we were able to grow most of our food. Both Yvonne and I spent many happy hours working in the garden. Number 48 was situated about half a mile or so from Home Farm. The farm was reached from a concrete track, also part of the air field and camp remains. It was Yvonne's practice to bring the two boys to the farm, if the weather permitted, while I was milking in the afternoon. On one occasion she had said to Tim, who was about two or so, we'll go and see Daddy in a minute, Tim decided that he wouldn't wait the minute and set off on his own. He arrived on his own, but closely followed by a very anxious and worried Mother.

It was my practice on hot days, only to wear shorts and wellies while milking in the afternoon. The reasons were several. It became very hot in a milking parlour with the sun streaming through the windows and ten very hot cows in close proximity. Clothing soon became wet and sticky and very uncomfortable. Also, during milking clothing became extremely "soiled," putting it politely. After milking had finished, it was easy to remove shorts and wellies and shower with the udder washers. It was on one of these occasions, that, whilst whistling and singing happily, at my ablutions, the farm managers two daughters arrived to collect their milk. I was completely engrossed and making quite a noise, so I didn't hear them until they were quite close. I made a rapid move to replace my shorts, and recover my dignity, the girls were very good, but as they left with their full can of milk, I thought that I heard some giggling. No! Surely not. On another occasion, I had stripped off enjoying my shower and I thought how disgusting the dairy towel was. I decided to give it a wash at the same time. I laid it on the floor and started to stamp on it squashing water and muck out. I don't know why, but I started to stamp up and down, and did an Indian war dance on it, making suitable Indian noises. Of course, as is inevitable, in came Ron. The look of amazement turned to a roar of laughter and it was a long time before he let me forget my Indian rain dance. When I think of it now, it must have been a life changing experience for him; I was stamping up and down on a wet towel, making groaning noises, without a stitch on. Oh well, of such experiences is life's rich tapestry woven.

After two and a half very enjoyable years at Home Farm, Tony became old enough to start school at Down Ampney School. I did mention earlier that the reports on the school weren't good. These reports turned out to be accurate. He wasn't enjoying the experience at all and really hated it. Yvonne and I began to think that we would have to take steps to remedy this situation soon and the sooner the better. In another year or so Tim would be starting school as well and we needed to start Tony in a school where he could learn and stay for a long period. This was important to me, as I had attended eight different schools and I'm sure this didn't enhance my education one little bit. I didn't want the boys to keep changing schools as I had done. It was while we were wondering what to do, that I was informed by the farm manager that a position of livestock supervisor needed to be filled. I had created a good impression with the farm manager at Down Ampney, and he had once said, possibly in an unguarded moment, that I was like a breath of spring. He suggested that I apply for the position, and that he would give me a good reference, although he hoped I didn't get it as he didn't want me to go. I took this as a great compliment.

Chapter Ten

Interview time again!

The position being offered was on the Co-operative estate at Weston Hall, Crewe, Cheshire. We hadn't lived so far north and we were a little concerned about the distance from our families, all on or close to the south coast. We calculated all the reasons to apply for the job, and all the reasons against it. Against applying were distance, location, no friends in that area and an unknown job for me that I may not like or be capable of tackling successfully. The reasons for were that it was a step up the ladder for me, better prospects, better remuneration, we had checked the school in Weston and it was a very good one, so that was another plus. We would also have free coal, rent, electricity, telephone and milk. All moving expenses would be paid and the house would be redecorated. The salary increase also meant that the pension would also increase. Taking everything into account, we really had to give it a go.

The interviews were arranged for February 1976, there were three of us from Down Ampney, one from the Weston Hall Estate and two others from Co-operative estates elsewhere in the country. We all collected nervously in the farm office and were introduced to each other. The interviewers were to be the ex assistant manager from Down Ampney, now taking over the managing of Weston Hall Estate and the manager from Down Ampney that had originally employed me. So these were familiar faces, and this did relax me somewhat. We were conducted round the various farms, six dairy units, a young stock unit and a small calf rearing unit. There were also 300 barley beef on the estate. The numbers of animals that the livestock supervisor would be responsible for were, 1200 milking cows, 2000 followers and 300 barley beef. This was a very great responsibility. The six dairy herds all had a foreman in charge and either two or three assistants. There was also an arable gang who were responsible for all field work including the silage making. The foremen on the dairy herds were a mixed lot and our reception was not very warm. They were responsible for their herd, anyone who was likely to start telling them what to do or how to do it, would not be welcome. Two of them were extremely hostile and the assistant manager who was taking our little group round was met with quite strong language. This was a little disturbing as at Down Ampney managers were called Mr Jones or whatever, it was unheard of for anyone to berate the management with oaths, and use their Christian name. Obviously a different approach was used here; it would take a little getting used to. We were taken round all the dairy farms, only a cursory glimpse really, there wasn't time for any in depth probing, so this would have to come at another time. The estate at Weston Hall was about 5000 acres, some of which was let. A majority of the dairies were bisected by the Crewe to London west coast train line. After a quick lunch we were taken to the house that went with the position. This was a modern semi-detached house with two bedrooms and a box room which was laughingly called the third bedroom. The garden was non existent and it was close beside the main farm entrance where all farm traffic entered and the dairy herd went passed four times a day. This was a far cry from our lovely house in Down Ampney, I could see that Yvonne wouldn't appreciate this move one little bit. Of course, I may not get the job, so it had to be a case of, trying my best, if Yvonne really didn't want to live here; I could turn the job down. I must admit, I wanted the challenge although I knew there would be tears and tantrums ahead. The interview went well, and although the farm manager asked how I would deal with having so many personnel to deal with. My experience was with only one man, was I capable. I replied that if I could get the best from Ron, then I was able to cope with most men. He gave a wry smile and gently nodded.

We all returned later that day, to face the inevitable questions, of what it had been like and did we know anything? Of course, we didn't and would have to wait. Yvonne asked what the house was like. I replied that there were lovely views from the lounge window. I think this did make her a little suspicious, but I was going to leave any more description of the house until I knew if I had been successful. It was about a week later that the assistant manager told me not to do much in the garden and winked at me. He didn't usually wink at me; he wasn't that sort of bloke, so I took it to mean that I was going to be told that I had got the job. Now the whole family would have to go to Crewe to view the property that we would move into and discuss the role that I would be expected to take on the Weston Hall Estate. It was now April, and if we were going to move, springtime is usually as good a time as any to do this. In the last week of April we all came to Crewe to finalise arrangements for me to be livestock supervisor. There hadn't been a livestock supervisor on this estate before, so it would be a new man in a new position that the foremen didn't want. Looking back I am amazed that we were accepted at all. Yvonne was not at all impressed with the house, a fact that I had been trying to ignore, but now had to be faced. The man in the other part of the semi-detached house was the unsuccessful applicant from Weston Hall for the job I was about to accept. Not a very good start for making friends. I enquired about any other properties that were owned by the estate and maybe suitable, but at that time there were none vacant. There was a possibility however that as some of the older workers retired, properties would be available and I could have first pick. Not an ideal situation, but it was the best we could hope for. We talked it over and Yvonne and I decided that because of the far improved educational facilities, we should accept the position. This we did and a date for moving was agreed. I had to give two weeks notice at Down Ampney, so the date was agreed on as 16th May 1976. A removal firm would collect our goods and chattels and take them to Crewe and unload them. This was to be the most civilised move we have ever made and we have had ten of these since our marriage! No tractor and trailer, no smelly cattle box, it was a dream and we arrived at Weston Hall as arranged.

It was much colder in Crewe than when we had left Cirencester three hours earlier. It was a sunny day, but there would be a frost that night. It was a strange year, spring had started very early, and silage making was already completed. We were now facing a very cold snap. For the first two weeks we had frosts every night and several falls of snow. We were beginning to wonder why we had moved so far north. On the 28th May, the frost disappeared and it became hot and sunny. We felt a little better. The estate was about nine miles long from the goods yard at Crewe Station to the little village of Woore. It took quite a while to locate the farms and especially the fields that were being used by young stock. Each dairy unit reared their own calves and looked after their own heifers. They were also responsible for getting heifers in calf and starting to produce milk. There is an optimum age for heifers to be when calving; at that time we usually expected them to be producing milk by two and a half to three years of age. The age range at Weston Hall was tremendous. The youngest were fine at two and a half, but the worst farm had heifers still not in calf at five years. I pointed out that we were loosing a great deal of money by feeding animals for two years longer than necessary, but the Forman just shrugged his shoulders and said that he liked them well grown. There was much work to do here.

Chapter Eleven
"Another fine mess I'd got myself into"

Now I had real responsibility. The Estate at Weston employed at that time fifty two men. These ranged from tractor drivers to cowmen to foremen, and down to the lowly G.F.W. (General Farm Worker). The assistant Farm Manager was responsible for the tractor drivers, and I was to be responsible for the dairy herds. There was more than a little animosity between the assistant farm manager and myself, because he had, up until the time I arrived, been responsible for the dairy herds as well as tractor drivers. He looked upon me as someone trying to take his job away from him. This didn't worry me excessively, as I was aware that assistant managers were moved to other estates frequently so as to give them as wide an experience as possible of the different estates and the different types of management. This duly occurred after a few months.

It was a difficult task to arrive on a new estate where there had been no Livestock Supervisor and make a place where I could fit in. I didn't want to be dictatorial, but I had to be firm. My first hurdle was the foremen on each dairy farm who had been used to doing everything as they wanted, so there were seven herds totalling eleven hundred milking cows all going there own way. The best did well, but the others were atrocious, barely breaking even financially. My job was to make the worst as good as the best and possibly make the best even better. No mean task when it involves seven different characters all thinking there way was the best. Where to start? I'm a tiny bit sad that at this time most of the humour disappeared out of my life for several years. It is easy to see how work pressure can affect a life so dramatically.

The job description was that the hours were to be like medicine, as and when necessary. I was a little too conscientious and didn't take any time off for three months. I had to be there to make sure everything was going the way it should be. This had two rather devastating effects, I became very tired and irritable, also Yvonne became very annoyed because I was tired and irritable and we never did anything together. Things came to a head one day, Yvonne could contain herself no longer and I was told a few things that I should have realised. I then started having alternate weekends off, but by this time the foremen had become so used to my always being there, that I would get telephone calls all the time. For self preservation, we would go out as much as possible, even if we only took the boys, a picnic and a cricket bat and ball and went to a quiet place on the estate.

Tony and Tim, my two boys aged 8 and 10 at Manor Farm

Our lovely Rusty dog. At Checkley

Chapter Twelve
Better Accomadation?

We were at Weston Hall Farm for about five years before a better house became available. I noticed it just after we moved to Weston, but a herdsman and his wife were living there. The house was large, six bedrooms, three reception and large farmhouse kitchen, it would be ideal for us. The property was in poor repair; the water had been coming through the roof for years and had caused a lot of damage. I asked the outgoing chap why he hadn't informed me that the bathroom roof was leaking. His reply? "If I'd said anything, you would only have moved the bath and put it under the leak." I must admit, that with so many properties to maintain, our builder was kept extremely busy. He had been, on more than one occasion, but his answer to a leaking flat roof was to cover it with plastic bags and coat it with cement, that lasted about two or three weeks and then the leak was back. Evidently on one occasion, the rain water had been running down the stairs.

When this house, Manor Farm, Blakenhall, had been vacated, I approached the estate manager, I enquired if we could inhabit said property. He thought for a bit and then said yes, but if any work needed doing, I must do it myself, but the estate would supply the materials. I readily agreed to this, it would be the best offer I would get. I took Yvonne and the lads to have a good look round; we hadn't been inside the house before. Well! A sorry sight met our eyes when we opened the back door. The draught from the open door caused the wallpaper all along the hallway, which was the full length of the house, to flap about. The paper was only held at the top. I commented, "Paper should strip easily." As we walked round, it was obvious that it had been a grand residence in its time, but it was certainly in a very sad state now. All the rooms needed decorating, some needed plastering as the plaster had come off with the paper. There was a bathroom, but taps didn't work, and the bath was stained with rust. The heating for the hot water supply was from a dilapidated York Range. There was one good living room and two good or passable bedrooms, so we could move in; this would make it easier to work on the place. Manor Farm was about four miles from where we were living at Weston, so the chances of going there after work were slim. If we lived in the house we could work every spare minute. BUT! Some things would have to be done before we moved in. The old range had to come out. I had found a second hand diesel fired cooker for sale. The manager agreed to purchase this if I fitted it. So this I did. I also found an excellent bathroom suite for sale and we agreed the same terms. The house was now habitable, so we moved in with furniture while I was still plumbing the hot water system. We used the farms Land Rover and cattle trailer to do this, in my own time.

We spent many hours, stripping wallpaper, scraping off a hundred and fifty years of distemper and plastering walls. As we progressed, we slowly moved into another room. It was extremely hard work, people thought we were mad to take on such a mammoth task, but there was great satisfaction as we slowly knocked the house into a habitable property. Oh! The garden, I forgot that. It was a wilderness, not touched for years, brambles, nettles and twenty years of weed growth. This we tackled on dry days, the house on wet ones, slowly it all came together. We lived at Manor Farm for about six years and it was a wonderful home. Since we left in 1986, Manor has been sold, modernised and enlarged and is now on the market at over two million pounds!

The boys had a wonderful time whilst we lived in this farmhouse. There were parties and revelry on many occasions and as the Manor was in the middle of a hundred acres of arable, there were no neighbours to disturb or to complain. One such party was arranged by Tony. I am not sure of the occasion, but about fifteen teenagers were invited. As Yvonne and I had to go out for a short while, we left them to their own devices. We had left lots of food, soft drinks, and two bottles of cider. This divided between sixteen, seemed fairly safe to us. When we arrived back, there were some very sorry looking teenagers waiting for us. Heads were in waste paper baskets, buckets, bowls and any other receptacle available. Unbeknown to us, one of the lads had brought in a bottle of gin and mixed it with cider. A very potent brew. They heaved and groaned until their parents arrived to collect them. We were worried sick, what would the other parents think of us, allowing this to happen? The kids were wonderful, they all got up from their various recumbent positions and walked out, politely saying "thank you" as they walked steadily to waiting cars. What troupers, there was hope for the next generation! No parental complaints were received, so we were in the clear.

All this time, while working on the house and garden, I had been developing the various herds on the estate and things were going well. All the herds were approaching a good standard now. Herdsmen were all working in the same manner and pulling together. Weston Hall was now one of the best estates and farmers were visiting by the coach load to see how it was done. Great? Well, you would think so. But no! As this estate was now doing so well, there would no longer be need for a Livestock Supervisor. Like so many others I was to be made redundant forthwith!

Chapter Thirteen
Reduncancy

This was a sledge hammer blow to Yvonne and I. We had worked so hard to get everything to run well and have a nice home and now this. At first, I was so upset that I only saw the negative side, but as time went by I saw another more positive side. For sometime, my eyesight had been deteriorating, I had always been very short sighted and now I had glaucoma. The Livestock Supervisors job entailed a massive amount of driving. To go to the six herds once was a round trip of twenty seven miles. I did this twice a day, and then there were trips for spares and repairs, this amounted to about four hundred miles a week, sometimes more. I'd had two recent driving accidents, so perhaps I should do a job with less road driving.

As one of the poorest herdsmen on the estate was leaving, I asked if I could go back to milking again. I never liked milking, but needs must. The herd that was being left was the poorest herd, so here again, I could only improve. This was agreed, and I think all were relieved, as no redundancy payment would be incurred. Oh! Whoopee! Another move. Both our lads had left or were about to leave school by now, so that would not be a problem. We had been able to keep their schooling going without a change of school. At least that was a goal achieved. I had built up a good rapport with the staff on the estate by this time and they were sad to see me leave my supervisory position. But, nothing can go on forever, so heads up, let's move on.

Chapter Fourteen
We Move to Checkley Wood Farm

As this move was a compulsory move and not one I had requested, I was able to get the large house at Checkley Wood, made pleasantly habitable. It was built with two floors. There were four bedrooms and a bathroom on the top floor, two reception and a self contained flat on the first floor, large kitchen and a reception room on the ground floor. The whole house was in need of modernising and decorating. This was all carried out by professionals before we moved in, much to our relief. We moved into Checkley on 5th October 1986, Yvonne's birthday. This time, a van was hired, so the move was quick and fairly painless.

I started work the following day. Back to milking cows again, not my favourite job. I had two assistants, so I didn't have to milk every day. There were just over two hundred cows in the Checkley herd, over one fifth of the estates production. The herd was not yielding well and the estate manager told me that I was to only have beef calves, as the cows were not good enough to have replacement milking cows. I used my own judgement and selected the best to have dairy calves. The herd was only yielding 4,500 litres when I took over, about one thousand gallons per cow. Not very good for this period. Checkley was the worst performing herd on the estate. Had I been here before? My first priority was to ensure that the cows had sufficient feed and were comfortable. If the best is wanted from them, you have to give them the best. My strategy worked and during the next six years the herd became one of the highest yielding in the country. We really enjoyed our time at Checkley Wood. On summer evenings we would take the two dogs and one Nanny goat for a walk down the drive, which was exactly one mile long. On our return we would sit on the top front door step with a glass of wine and watch the glowing ball of the sun, go down over the wood. Of such simple pleasures are memories made. We had worked hard on the garden, reclaiming it from the field. God was in his Heaven, all's right with the world. He then had other ideas. My eyesight, which had still been deteriorating, was getting quite bad. On my most recent visit for a check-up, I was told that it was really too dangerous to be working with cows. I had already stopped driving. I ignored the advice at the time, but I realised that I was getting injured more, because I wasn't quick enough to avoid a fast moving animal. I'd received a broken hand and very bruised ribs while milking. At my next visit to the consultant, he asked if I was still working. When I told him that I was still working he was a bit miffed. "Right" he said, "I am giving you a letter and a sick note, you must stop today." That was it, working life over, 52 years old. The farm manager was not best pleased, this was not in his plans, but there was not a lot I could do. We now had to vacate Checkley Wood Farm house.

The Co-operative Agricultural Group had a policy, at the time, of being able to accommodate retired workers in a Co-op house. This was because they had many empty houses. We now required a house near a bus route and able to accommodate all four of us. The boys were still at home and were not about to leave in the immediate future. There was a property on the main road in Wrinehill, about two miles away. It had been a smallholding, but the land had been taken back in hand when the tenant had died. The house had been empty for several years so was more or less derelict. It was agreed that the house would be made habitable before we moved in. We moved into Malt Kiln Farm on 5th October 1992. Yvonne's birthday, again!

Chapter Fifteen
Malt Kiln Farm, Wrinehill

After we had been at Malt Kiln a couple of months, I received a letter from the Queen. My first thought was, "what have I done wrong now, this must be serious." Wonder of wonders, the Co-op had put my name forward to receive a British Empire Medal, in the New Years Honours List, for my service to the estate and in recognition of charity work we had carried out over the years. To say that I was surprised would be a great understatement. I wrote back and said that I would accept the Honour. I received the medal later and Yvonne and I were invited to a garden party at Buckingham Palace. What excitement!

When I last visited the eye clinic, I was told that my sight would most likely last about another five years. Scary, but I had several years to get used to the idea. Moving to Malt Kiln was our last move, we would be left in peace to get used to the layout of the place and so be able to cope as vision decreased. Yvonne also had poor vision, so we were both able to understand each others problems. Here we were again, another house another garden. The "garden" consisted of three quarters of an acre. Most of it was either a building site or a stack yard. Nothing had been grown in it for ten years or more and the builders, who had renovated the house, had covered a large amount with house bricks, broken tiles and many other bits and pieces. We first cleared all the rubbish and then purchased three hundred privet bushes; we were here for the long term. We also laid five hundred square metres of lawn. We planted an orchard, made trellis, built walls and made Malt Kiln Farm a pleasant place to live. Everything took much longer than normal, as a lot of the work had to be attempted several times before I got it right. My sight was still getting worse. I opened up a long disused well, built a brick surround and made a roof for it. I had two green houses, and I much enjoyed making hanging baskets which I was able to sell on the garage forecourt opposite the house. We also sold vegetables and plants. All the money taken was ploughed back into the garden. I built a water feature with water from the well circulating through it. We had flowers and hanging baskets everywhere. Friends were invited for barbeques and God was back in His Heaven. My sigh, luckily, did not deteriorate at the suggested rate. Yes, it was certainly getting worse, but I could still cope fifteen years later. This was the time when we were approached by the estate agents that were now managing Co-op agriculture, to say that Malt Kiln was now to be sold and we must vacate the property. Not again! Since the Co-op had supplied our accommodation after I retired, they must still find us suitable accommodation. My sight was now in a poor state and we didn't want to move again. It appears that there is no obligation on the part of our landlord to keep us in the same house, so long as a suitable alternative is offered. To cut a long story short, a property was found in Betley in Rodger Avenue. This is three bed roomed, semi-detached property, ex council house with a very small garden at the back and not much at the front. I would certainly miss our lovely garden at Malt Kiln. However, the garden was getting a bit too much for me, so, all in all, it could be a good thing. We would be in the middle of the village of Betley; we knew a lot of people in the village and I had recently become involved with maintaining the I.T. equipment in the meeting room. So, on the 5th of October 2007, we moved to Rodger Avenue. Yvonne's birthday yet again.

During our stay at Malt Kiln, I had been asked by my friend who lived opposite us, if I would take a part in the local amateur dramatic Christmas panto. I played Postman Pat. I thoroughly enjoyed the experience, (always was a show off!) This was in 2005 and I have acted in a production once or twice every year until 2014. I played many parts, in plays and pantomime, I must admit, playing the Dame in panto's is great fun, but hard work. There is a great feeling of satisfaction if you "pull it off."

Yvonne and I 1996

Chapter sixteen
Rodger Avenue, Betley

All our friends had helped us move to Rodger Avenue, and many hands had made light work. We had little or no gardening to do, just a small lawn to cut occasionally. We decided to do the things we had always wanted to, while we could still manage.

We had, in the conservatory at Malt Kiln, a large picture of Lake Malign in Canada. We had always looked longingly at this, and sighed, "one day, one day." We decided that the one day had arrived, so

we booked up to cross Canada east to west, see
Niagara Falls and Lake Louise, cross the Rockies on
the Rocky Mountaineer, see Butchart Gardens and
then take a cruise from Vancouver to Glacier Bay and
back. Most enjoyable! We have also been to Corsica
and Sardinia. Another place I had wanted to see for
many years.

I also write, what I think are, witty ditties,
mostly one pagers, one of which I relate below. It
covers the memoirs that you have just been reading,
so if you had read this first, you need not have had to
read the whole book!

My Ode   Monologue

In 39 a boy was born, he was a funny chap,

His Mother said "He wasn't planned, he was a pure mishap"

His Father said in whispered tones "I don't think I agree,

I've been trying very hard, since 1933"

Father then he went to war; to fight for what was right

Leaving Mum to teach the lad and show him wrong from right.

Times they were not easy in war torn English streets

But, the lad, he made the grade, and then his Dad he greets.

The Lad was 6 and quite unsure of whom this man could be

But Mum embraced with open arms and gave him lots of tea.

They really seemed quite friendly as he ate up all our bread

And then when nigh time came around he slept in Mummy's bed.

Father then he bought some land that was so very rough,

We grew taters in this land but that was not enough.

30 goats were then acquired to help make our ends meet,

One of these did not like me and chased me down the street.

Times improved, a house was built the land became a farm,

And I helped Dad, I worked so hard but didn't come to harm.

3 years went by, the farm was sold a larger one was bought

I played with calves and pigs and lambs and things I shouldn't ought.

The land was good, we did well and I enjoyed my school

At 13 years of age my friends I thought I was so cool

At this time of joy and fun I really could have cried

When we were told at the school that our dear King had died.

At this time we moved again a larger farm required

The Forest of Dean was the chosen spot and so a farm acquired,

The land was steep as steep can be, the cattle began to run,

There was no hope of stopping them till they'd had their fun

Charging down the hill so steep at 90 miles an hour,

They could not stop or slow down they were a proper shower,

The river stopped them, I'm glad to say, it was to our relief,

But fences they will not withstand 20 tons of beef.

I left school and worked full time with my brother and my Dad,

Just 15years and knew it all, it was so very sad

We worked hard through night and day just to make ends meet

We grew veg to help the funds, but this the rabbits did eat.

The farm was sold we moved to Devon, where farms were cheap as marg.

180 acres or so, it seemed so very large,

The house was thatched with walls of mud that really had past their best

The walls caved in one winters night, I ran out in my vest.

Water came from a well, we had no electric light

Oil lamps and candles were what we used at night

The toilet it was basic, and used by all about

But just remember what goes in must be emptied out.

Things went well, a house was built, electric came to stay

We had 100 cows or more, but had no time to play,

My brother he got married, it really was unfair,

We both agreed that we should try and get some work elsewhere.

At this time I had a pain, it was appendicitis

They took me in and whipped it out, but this did not delight us.

But while this job was being done, and I was stuck in bed

I espied a pretty nurse and we did soon get wed.

Oh! Good grief, what had I done? There was no turning back,

Married life was not the same; I had to learn the knack,

But with time and practice, we really did work well

Two little boys soon came along; I must have rung the bell.

We then moved to Down Ampney, to work a Co-op farm,

3 years we stayed and worked so hard but didn't come to harm.

In 75 we moved again to further my career,

We came north to Cheshire, it seemed a good idea.

Now we've been here for many years, we've made a
lot of friends,

Some of them are reading this, I hope I won't offend.

In Betley now we've made our home, and this is
where we'll stay,

Trying hard to do our bit and pass our time away.

When I finished on the farm, I was given a gong,

British Empire Medal indeed, was the short and long.

It was nice when work was done, to think that
someone cared,

And appreciated what I'd done, and this to the Queen
had shared.

So my friends I bid you well, as I end my little ditty,

I have tried to make it true, and also make it witty.

Farewell to one and all I say, I maybe back some time,

Until then I wave goodbye, and now I end my rhyme.

Printed in Great Britain
by Amazon.co.uk, Ltd.,
Marston Gate.